P9-DGV-088

INTERNATIONAL

THE
DROWNED
AND
THE
SAVED

PRIMO LEVI

THE DROWNED AND THE SAVED

TRANSLATED FROM THE ITALIAN BY RAYMOND ROSENTHAL

VINTAGE INTERNATIONAL

VINTAGE BOOKS

A DIVISION OF RANDOM HOUSE, INC.

NEW YORK

First Vintage International Edition, April 1989

Translation copyright © 1988 Simon & Schuster, Inc.

All rights reserved under International and Pan-American Copyright Conventions. Published in the United States by Random House, Inc., New York. Originally published in Italian as *Sommersi e i salvati* by Giulio Einaudi editore s.p.a., Torino, in 1986. Copyright © 1986 by Giulio Einaudi editore s.p.a., Torino. This translation originally published, in hardcover, by Summit Books, a division of Simon & Schuster, Inc., in 1988.

Library of Congress Cataloging-in-Publication Data
Levi, Primo.
    The drowned and the saved.
    Reprint. Originally published: New York:
Summit Books, © 1988.
    Translation of: I Sommersi e i salvati.
    1. Holocaust, Jewish (1939–1945)–Personal
narratives.   2. Auschwitz (Poland: Concentration
camp)   3. Levi, Primo.   4. Authors, Italian–20th
century–Biography.   I. Title.
D804.3.L4813   1989   940.53'15'0392404386   88-40375
ISBN 0-679-72186-X (pbk.)

Manufactured in the United States of America
79B86

Since then, at an uncertain hour,
That agony returns,
And till my ghastly tale is told
This heart within me burns.

SAMUEL TAYLOR COLERIDGE
The Rime of the Ancient Mariner
vv. 582–85

CONTENTS

PREFACE

THE first news about the Nazi annihilation camps began to spread in the crucial year of 1942. They were vague pieces of information, yet in agreement with each other: they delineated a massacre of such vast proportions, of such extreme cruelty and such intricate motivation that the public was inclined to reject them because of their very enormity. It is significant that the culprits themselves foresaw this rejection well in advance: many survivors (among others, Simon Wiesenthal in the last pages of *The Murderers Are Among Us*) remember that the SS militiamen enjoyed cynically admonishing the prisoners:

> However this war may end, we have won the war against you; none of you will be left to bear witness, but even if someone were to survive, the world will not believe him. There will perhaps be suspicions, discussions, research by historians, but there will be no certainties, because we will destroy the evidence together with you. And even if some proof should remain and some of you survive, people will say that the events you describe are too monstrous to be

believed: they will say that they are the exaggerations of Allied propaganda and will believe us, who will deny everything, and not you. We will be the ones to dictate the history of the Lagers.

Strangely enough, this same thought ("even if we were to tell it, we would not be believed") arose in the form of nocturnal dreams produced by the prisoners' despair. Almost all the survivors, orally or in their written memoirs, remember a dream which frequently recurred during the nights of imprisonment, varied in its detail but uniform in its substance: they had returned home and with passion and relief were describing their past sufferings, addressing themselves to a loved one, and were not believed, indeed were not even listened to. In the most typical (and cruelest) form, the interlocutor turned and left in silence. This is a theme to which we shall return, but at this point it is important to emphasize how both parties, victims and oppressors, had a keen awareness of the enormity and therefore the noncredibility of what took place in the Lagers—and, we may add here, not only in the Lagers, but in the ghettos, in the rear areas of the Eastern front, in the police stations, and in the asylums for the mentally handicapped.

Fortunately, things did not go as the victims feared and the Nazis hoped. Even the most perfect of organizations has its flaws, and Hitler's Germany, especially during the last months before the collapse, was far from being a perfect machine. Much material evidence of the mass exterminations was suppressed, or a more or less dextrous attempt was made to suppress it: in the autumn of 1944 the Nazis blew up the gas chambers and crematoria at Auschwitz, but the ruins are still there, and despite the contortions of epigones it is difficult to justify their function by having recourse to fanciful hypotheses. The Warsaw ghetto, after the famous insurrection in the spring of 1943, was razed to the ground, but thanks to the superhuman concern of a number of fighter-historians (historians of themselves!), in the rubble, often many meters deep, or smuggled beyond the wall, other historians would later rediscover the testimony of how the ghetto lived and died day by day. All the archives in the Lagers were burned during the final days of the war, truly an irremediable loss, so that even today there is discussion as to whether the victims were four, six, or eight million—although one still talks of millions. Before the Nazis had recourse to the gigantic multiple crematoria, the innumerable corpses of the victims, deliberately killed or worn down by hardship and illness, could have constituted evidence and somehow had to be made to disappear. The first solution, macabre to the point of making one hesitate to speak of it, had been simply to pile up the bodies, hundreds of thousands of bodies, in huge common graves, and this was done, in particular at Treblinka and other minor Lagers, and in the wake of the German army in Russia. This was a temporary solution decided upon with bestial insouciance when the German armies were winning on all fronts and final victory appeared certain: they would decide afterward what should be done, and in any case the victor is the master even of truth, can manipulate it as he pleases. Somehow the common graves would be justified, or made to disappear, or attributed to the Soviets (who, for that matter, proved at Katyn not to be lagging too far behind). But after Stalingrad there were second thoughts: best to erase everything immediately. The prisoners themselves were forced to exhume those pitiful remains and burn them on pyres in the open, as if so unusual an operation of such proportions could go completely unnoticed.

The SS command posts and the security services then took the greatest care to ensure that no witness survived. This is the meaning (it would be difficult to excogitate another) of the murderous and apparently insane transfers with which the history of the Nazi camps came to an end during the first months of 1945: the survivors of Maidanek to Auschwitz, those of Auschwitz to Buchenwald and Mauthausen, those of Buchenwald to Bergen-Belsen, the women of Ravensbrück to Schwerin. In short, everyone had to be snatched away from liberation, deported again to the heart of a Germany that was being invaded from the west and east. It did not matter that they might die along the way; what really mattered was that they should not tell their story. In fact, after having functioned as centers of political terror, then as death factories, and subsequently (or simultaneously) as immense, ever renewed reservoirs of slave labor, the Lagers had become dangerous for a moribund Germany because they contained the secret of the Lagers themselves, the greatest crime in the history of humanity. The army of ghosts that still vegetated in them was composed of *Geheimnisfräger*, the bearers of secrets who must be disposed of; the extermination plants, also very eloquent, having been destroyed, had to be moved to the interior, it was decided, in the absurd hope of still being able to lock those ghosts up in Lagers less threatened by the advancing fronts and to exploit their final ability to work, and in the other, less absurd hope that the torment of those Biblical marches would reduce their number. And in fact their number was appallingly reduced, yet some nevertheless had the luck or the strength to survive and remained to bear witness.

Less well known and less studied is the fact that many bearers of secrets were also on the other side, although many knew little and few knew everything. No one will ever be able to establish with precision how many, in the Nazi apparatus, could *not not know* about the frightful atrocities being committed, how many knew something but were in a position to pretend that they did not know, and, further, how many had the possibility of knowing everything but chose the more prudent path of keeping their eyes and ears (and above all their mouths) well shut. Whatever the case, since one cannot suppose that the majority of Germans lightheartedly accepted the slaughter, it is certain that the failure to divulge the truth about the Lagers represents one of the major collective crimes of the German people and the most obvious demonstration of the cowardice to which Hitlerian terror had reduced them: a cowardice which became an integral part of mores and so profound as to prevent husbands from telling their wives, parents their children. Without this cowardice the greatest excesses would not have been carried out, and Europe and the world would be different today.

Without a doubt those who knew the horrible truth because they were (or had been) responsible had compelling reasons to remain silent; but inasmuch as they were depositories of the secret, even by keeping silent they could not always be sure of remaining alive, witness the case of Stangl and the other Treblinka butchers, who after the insurrection there and the dismantling of that Lager were transferred to one of the most dangerous Partisan areas.

Willed ignorance and fear also led many potential "civilian" witnesses of the infamies of the Lagers to remain silent. Especially during the last years of the war, the Lagers constituted an extensive and complex system which profoundly compenetrated the daily life of the country; one has with good reason spoken of the *univers concentrationnaire*, but it was not a closed universe. Small and large industrial companies, agricultural combines, agencies, and arms factories drew profits from the practically free labor supplied by the camps. Some exploited the prisoners pitilessly, accepting the inhuman (and also stupid) principle of the SS according to which one prisoner was worth another, and if the work killed him he could immediately be replaced; others, a few, cautiously tried to alleviate their sufferings. Still other industries—or perhaps the same ones—made money by supplying the Lagers themselves: lumber, building materials, cloth for the prisoners' striped uniforms, dehydrated vegetables for the soup, etc. The crematoria ovens themselves were designed, built, assembled, and tested by a German company, Topf of Wiesbaden (it was still in operation in 1975, building crematoria for civilian use, and had not considered the advisability of changing its name). It is hard to believe that the personnel of these companies did not realize the significance of the quality or quantity of the merchandise and installations being commissioned by the SS command units. The same can be, and has been, said with regard to the supplies of the poison employed in the gas chambers at Auschwitz: the product, substantially hydrocyanic acid, had already been used for many years for pest control in the holds of boats, but the abrupt increase in orders beginning with 1942 could scarcely go unnoticed. It must have aroused doubts, and certainly did, but they were stifled by fear, the desire for profit, the blindness and willed stupidity that we have mentioned, and in some cases (probably few) by fanatical Nazi obedience.

It is natural and obvious that the most substantial material for the reconstruction of truth about the camps is the memories of the survivors. Beyond the pity and indignation these recollections provoke, they should also be read with a critical eye. For knowledge of the Lagers, the Lagers themselves were not always a good observation post: in the inhuman conditions to which they were subjected, the prisoners could barely acquire an overall vision of their universe. The prisoners, above all those who did not understand German, might not even know where in Europe their Lager was situated, having arrived after a slaughterous and tortuous journey in sealed boxcars. They did not know about the existence of other Lagers, even those only a few kilometers away. They did not know for whom they worked. They did not understand the significance of certain sudden changes in conditions, or of the mass transfers. Surrounded by death, the deportee was often in no position to evaluate the extent of the slaughter unfolding before his eyes. The companion who worked beside him today was gone by the morrow: he might be in the hut next door, or erased from the world; there was no way to know. In short, the prisoner felt overwhelmed by a massive edifice of violence and menace but could not form for himself a representation of it because his eyes were fixed to the ground by every single minute's needs.

This deficiency conditioned the oral or written testimonies of the "normal" prisoners, those not privileged, who represented the core of the camps and who escaped death only by a combination of improbable events. They were the majority in the Lager, but an exiguous minority among the survivors: among them, those who during their imprisonment enjoyed some sort of privilege are much more numerous. At a distance of years one can today definitely affirm that the history of the Lagers has been written almost exclusively by those who, like myself, never fathomed them to the bottom. Those who did so did not return, or their capacity for observation was paralyzed by suffering and incomprehension.

On the other hand, the "privileged" witnesses could avail themselves of a certainly better observatory, if only because it was higher up and hence took in a more extensive horizon; but it was to a greater or lesser degree also falsified by the privilege itself. The discussion concerning privilege (not only in the Lager) is delicate, and I shall try to go into it later with the greatest possible objectivity. Here I will only mention the fact that the privileged par excellence, that is, those who acquired privilege for themselves by becoming subservient to the camp authority, did not bear witness at all, for obvious reasons, or left incomplete or distorted or totally false testimony. Therefore the best historians of the Lagers emerged from among the very few who had the ability and luck to attain a privileged observatory without bowing to compromises, and the skill to tell what they saw, suffered, and did with the humility of a good chronicler, that is, taking into account the complexity of the Lager phenomenon and the variety of human destinies being played out in it. It was in the logic of things that these historians should almost all be political prisoners: because the Lagers were a political phenomenon; because the political prisoners, much more than the Jews and the criminals (as we know, the three principal categories of prisoners), disposed of a cultural background which allowed them to interpret the events they saw; and because, precisely inasmuch as they were ex-combatants or antifascist combatants even now, they realized that testimony was an act of war against fascism; because they had easier access to statistical data; and lastly, because often, besides holding important positions in the Lager, they were members of the secret defense organization. At least during the final years, their living conditions were tolerable, which permitted them, for example, to write and preserve notes, an unthinkable luxury for the Jews and a possibility of no interest to the criminals.

For all the reasons touched on here, the truth about the Lagers has come to light down a long road and through a narrow door, and many aspects of the *univers concentrationnaire* have yet to be explored in depth. By now more than forty years have passed since the liberation of the Nazi Lagers; this considerable interval has, for the purposes of clarification, led to conflicting results, which I will try to enumerate.

In the first place, there has been the decanting, a desirable and normal process, thanks to which historical events acquire their chiaroscuro and perspective only some decades after their conclusion. At the end of World War II, quantitative data on the Nazi deportations and massacres, in the Lagers and elsewhere, had not been acquired, nor was it easy to understand their import and specificity. For only a few years now has one begun to understand that the Nazi slaughter was dreadfully "exemplary" and that, if nothing worse happens in the coming years, it will be remembered as the central event, the scourge, of this century.

By contrast, the passage of time has as a consequence other historically negative results. The greater part of the witnesses, for the defense and the prosecution, have by now disappeared, and those who remain, and who (overcoming their remorse or, alternately, their wounds) still agree to testify, have ever more blurred and stylized memories, often, unbeknownst to them, influenced by information gained from later readings or the stories of others. In some cases, naturally, the lack of memory is simulated, but the many years that have gone by make it credible. Also, the "I don't know" or " I did not know" spoken today by many

Germans no longer shocks us, as it did or should have when events were recent.

Of another or further stylization we are ourselves responsible, we survivors, or, more precisely, those among us who have decided to live our condition as survivors in the simplest and least critical way. This does not mean that ceremonies and celebrations, monuments and flags are always and everywhere to be deplored. A certain dose of rhetoric is perhaps indispensable for the memory to persist. That sepulchres, "the urns of the strong," kindle souls to perform lofty deeds, or at least preserve the memory of accomplished deeds, was true in Foscolo's time and is still true today; but one must beware of oversimplifications. Every victim is to be mourned, and every survivor is to be helped and pitied, but not all their acts should be set forth as examples. The inside of the Lager was an intricate and stratified microcosm; the "gray zone" of which I shall speak later, that of the prisoners who in some measure, perhaps with good intentions, collaborated with the authority, was not negligible. Indeed, it constituted a phenomenon of fundamental importance for the historian, the psychologist, and the sociologist. There is not a prisoner who does not remember this and who does not remember his amazement at the time: the first threats, the first insults, the first blows came not from the SS but from other prisoners, from "colleagues," from those mysterious personages who nevertheless wore the same striped tunic that they, the new arrivals, had just put on. This book means to contribute to the clarification of some aspects of the Lager phenomenon which still appear obscure. It also sets itself a more ambitious goal, to try to answer the most urgent question, the question which torments all those who have happened to read our accounts: How much of the concentration camp world is dead and will not return, like slavery and the dueling code? How much is back or is coming back? What can each of us do so that in this world pregnant with threats at least this threat will be nullified?

I did not intend, nor would I have been able, to do a historian's work, that is, exhaustively examine the sources. I have almost exclusively confined myself to the National Socialist Lagers because I had direct experience only of these; I also have had copious indirect experience of them, through books read, stories listened to, and encounters with the readers of my first two books. Besides, up to the moment of this writing, and notwithstanding the horror of Hiroshima and Nagasaki, the shame of the Gulags, the useless and bloody Vietnam War, the Cambodian self-genocide, the *desaparecidos* of Argentina, and the many atrocious and stupid wars we have seen since, the Nazi concentration camp system still remains a *unicum*, both in its extent and its quality. At no other place or time has one seen a phenomenon so unexpected and so complex: never have so many human lives been extinguished in so short a time, and with so lucid a combination of technological ingenuity, fanaticism, and cruelty. No one wants to absolve the Spanish conquistadors of the massacres perpetrated in the Americas throughout the sixteenth century. It seems they brought about the death of at least sixty million Indios; but they acted on their own, without or against the directives of their government, and they diluted their misdeeds—not very "planned" to tell the truth—over an arc of more than one hundred years, and they were also helped by the epidemics that they inadvertently brought with them. And, finally, have we not tried to dispose of them by declaring that they were "things of another time"?

1

THE MEMORY
OF THE OFFENSE

HUMAN memory is a marvelous but fallacious instrument. This is a threadbare truth known not only to psychologists but also to anyone who has paid attention to the behavior of those who surround him, or even to his own behavior. The memories which lie within us are not carved in stone; not only do they tend to become erased as the years go by, but often they change, or even grow, by incorporating extraneous features. Judges know this very well: almost never do two eyewitnesses of the same event describe it in the same way and with the same words, even if the event is recent and if neither of them has a personal interest in distorting it. This scant reliability of our memories will be satisfactorily explained only when we know in what language, in what alphabet they are written, on what surface, and with what pen: to this day we are still far from this goal. Some mechanisms are known which falsify memory under particular conditions: traumas, not only cerebral ones; interference from other "competitive" memories; abnormal conditions of consciousness; repressions; blockages.

23

Nevertheless, even under normal conditions a slow degradation is at work, an obfuscation of outlines, a so to speak physiological oblivion, which few memories resist. Doubtless one may discern here one of the great powers of nature, the same that degrades order into disorder, youth into old age, and extinguishes life in death. Certainly practice (in this case, frequent re-evocation) keeps memories fresh and alive in the same manner in which a muscle often used remains efficient, but it is also true that a memory evoked too often, and expressed in the form of a story, tends to become fixed in a stereotype, in a form tested by experience, crystallized, perfected, adorned, installing itself in the place of the raw memory and growing at its expense.

I intend to examine here the memories of extreme experiences, of injuries suffered or inflicted. In this case, all or almost all the factors that can obliterate or deform the mnemonic record are at work: the memory of a trauma suffered or inflicted is itself traumatic because recalling it is painful or at least disturbing. A person who has been wounded tends to block out the memory so as not to renew the pain; the person who has inflicted the wound pushes the memory deep down, to be rid of it, to alleviate the feeling of guilt.

Here, as with other phenomena, we are dealing with a paradoxical analogy between victim and oppressor, and we are anxious to be clear: both are in the same trap, but it is the oppressor, and he alone, who has prepared it and activated it, and if he suffers from this, it is right that he should suffer; and it is iniquitous that the victim should suffer from it, as he does indeed suffer from it, even at a distance of decades. Once again it must be observed, mournfully, that the injury cannot be healed: it extends through time, and the Furies, in whose existence we are forced to believe, not only rack the tormentor (if they do rack him, assisted or not by human punishment), but perpetuate the tormentor's work by denying peace to the tormented. It is not without horror that we read the words left us by Jean Améry, the Austrian philosopher tortured by the Gestapo because he was active in the Belgian resistance and then deported to Auschwitz because he was Jewish:

> Anyone who has been tortured remains tortured. . . .
> Anyone who has suffered torture never again will be able to be at ease in the world, the abomination of the annihilation is never extinguished. Faith in humanity, already cracked by the first slap in the face, then demolished by torture, is never acquired again.

Torture was for him an interminable death: Améry, about whom I will speak again in Chapter 6, killed himself in 1978.

We do not wish to abet confusions, small-change Freudianism, morbidities, or indulgences. The oppressor remains what he is, and so does the victim. They are not interchangeable. The former is to be punished and execrated (but, if possible, understood), the latter is to be pitied and helped; but both, faced by the indecency of the irrevocable act, need refuge and protection, and instinctively search for them. Not all, but most—and often for their entire lives.

By now we are in possession of numerous confessions, depositions, and admissions on the part of the oppressors (I speak not only of the German National Socialists but of all those who commit horrendous and multiple crimes in obedience to a discipline): some given in court, others during interviews, others still contained in books or memoirs. In my opinion, these are documents of the utmost importance. In general, the descriptions of the things seen and the acts committed are of little interest: they amply coincide with what victims have recounted; very rarely are they contested; judgments have been handed down and they are by now part of history. Often they are regarded as well known. Much more important are the motivations and justifications: Why did you do this? Were you aware that you were committing a crime?

The answers to these two questions, or to others which are analogous, are very similar to each other, independently of the personality of the interrogated person, be he an ambitious and intelligent professional like Speer or a gelid fanatic like Eichmann, a short-sighted functionary like Stangl in Treblinka or Höss in Auschwitz, or an obtuse brute like Boger or Kaduk, the inventors of torture. Expressed in different formulations and with greater or lesser arrogance, depending on the speaker's mental and cultural level, in the end they substantially all say the same things: I did it because I was ordered to; others (my superiors) have committed acts worse than mine; in view of the upbringing I received, and the environment in which I lived, I could not have acted differently; had I not done it, another would have done it even more harshly in my place. For anyone who reads these justifications the first reaction is revulsion: they lie, they cannot believe they will be believed, they cannot not see the imbalance between their excuses and the enormity of pain and death they have caused. They lie knowing that they are lying: they are in bad faith.

Now, anyone who has sufficient experience of human affairs knows that the distinction (the opposition, a linguist would say) good faith/bad faith is optimistic and smacks of the Enlightenment, and is all the more so, and for much greater reason, when applied to men such as those just mentioned. It presupposes a mental clarity which few have and which even these few immediately lose when, for whatever reason, past or present reality arouses anxiety or discomfort in them. Under such conditions there are, it is true, those who lie consciously, coldly falsifying reality itself, but more numerous are those who weigh anchor, move off, momentarily or forever, from genuine memories, and fabricate for themselves a convenient reality. The past is a burden to them; they feel repugnance for things done or suffered and tend to replace them with others. The substitution may begin in full awareness, with an invented scenario, mendacious, restored, but less painful than the real one; they repeat the description to others but also to themselves, and the distinction between true and false progressively loses its contours, and man ends by fully believing the story he has told so many times and continues to tell, polishing and retouching here and there the details which are least credible or incongruous or incompatible with the acquired picture of historically accepted events: initial bad faith has become good faith. The silent transition from falsehood to self-deception is useful: anyone who lies in good faith is better off. He recites his part better, is more easily believed by the judge, the historian, the reader, his wife, and his children.

The further events fade into the past, the more the construction of convenient truth grows and is perfected. I believe that only by this mental mechanism is it possible to interpret, for instance, the statements made in 1978 to *L'Express* by Louis Darquier de Pellepoix, former commissioner of Jewish affairs in the Vichy government around 1942, and as such personally responsible for the deportation of seventy thousand Jews. Darquier denies everything: the photographs of piles of corpses are montages; the statistics of millions of dead were fabricated by the Jews, always greedy for publicity, commiseration, and indemnities: there may perhaps have been deportations (he would have found it difficult to dispute them: his signature appears at the foot of too many letters giving orders for these very deportations, even of children), but he did not know where to or with what results; there were, it is true, gas chambers in Auschwitz, but only to kill lice, and anyway (note the coherence!) they were built for propaganda purposes after the end of the war. It is not my intention to justify this cowardly and foolish man, and it offends me to know that he lived for a long time undisturbed in Spain, but I think I can recognize in him the typical case of someone who, accustomed to lying in public, ends by lying in private, too, to himself as well, and building for himself a comforting truth which allows him to live in peace. To keep good and bad faith distinct costs a lot: it requires a decent sincerity or truthfulness with oneself; it demands a continuous intellectual and moral effort. How can such an effort be expected from men like Darquier?

Reading the statements made by Eichmann during the Jerusalem trial, and those of Rudolph Höss (the penultimate commander of Auschwitz, the inventor of the hydrocyanic acid chambers) in his autobiography, one can see in them a process of re-elaboration of the past, more subtle than Darquier's. In substance, these two defended themselves in the classical manner of the Nazi militia, or, better yet, of all militiamen: we have been educated in absolute obedience, hierarchy, nationalism; we have been imbued with slogans, intoxicated with ceremonies and demonstrations; we have been taught that the only justice was that which was to the advantage of our people and that the only truth was the words of the Leader. What do you want from us? How can you even think to expect from us, after the fact, a behavior different from ours and that of all those who were like us? We were the diligent executors, and for our diligence we were praised and promoted. The decisions were not ours because the regime in which we grew up did not permit autonomous decisions: others have decided for us, and that was the only way it could have happened because our ability to decide had been amputated. Therefore we are not responsible and cannot be punished.

Even projected against the background of the Birkenau smokestacks, this reasoning cannot be considered purely the fruit of impudence. The pressure that a modern totalitarian state can exercise over the individual is frightful. Its weapons are substantially three: direct propaganda or propaganda camouflaged as upbringing, instruction, and popular culture; the barrier erected against pluralism of information; and terror. Nevertheless, it is not permissible to admit that this pressure is irresistible, especially in the brief twelve-year term of the Third Reich. In the affirmations and exculpations of men responsible for such serious crimes as were Höss and Eichmann, the exaggeration and, to an even greater degree, the manipulation of memory is obvious. Both were born and raised long before the Reich became truly "totalitarian," and their joining the Nazi party was a choice dictated more by opportunism than enthusiasm. The re-elaboration of their past was a later work, slow and (probably) not methodical. To ask oneself whether it was done in good or bad faith is naive. They too, so strong in the face of others' suffering, when fate put them before judges, before the death they deserved, built a convenient past for themselves and ended by believing in it, espcially Höss, who was not a subtle man. As he appears in his writings, he was in fact a person so little inclined to self-control and introspection that he does not realize he is confirming his coarse anti-Semitism by the very act in which he abjures and denies it, nor does he realize how slimy his self-portrait as a good functionary, father, and husband actually is.

As a comment on these reconstructions of the past (but not only on these: it is an observation that holds for all memories) one must note that the distortion of fact is often limited by the objectivity of the facts themselves, around which there exists the testimonies of third parties, documents, *corpora delicti*, historically accepted contexts. It is generally difficult to deny having committed a given act, or that such an act was committed; it is, on the contrary, very easy to alter the motivations which led us to an act and the passions within us which accompanied the act itself. This is an extremely fluid matter, subject to distortion even under very weak pressure; to the questions Why did you do this? or What were you thinking as you did it? no reliable answers exist, because states of mind are by nature labile and even more labile is the memory of them.

An extreme case of the distortion of the memory of a committed guilty act is found in its suppression. Here, too, the borderline between good and bad faith can be vague; behind the "I don't know" and the "I do not remember" that one hears in courtrooms there is sometimes the precise intent to lie, but at other times it is a fossilized lie, rigidified in a formula. The rememberer has decided not to remember and has succeeded: by dint of denying its existence, he has expelled the harmful memory as one expels an excretion or a parasite. Lawyers for the defense know very well that the memory gap, or the putative truth, which they suggest to their clients, tends to become forgetfulness and the actual truth. It is not necessary to trespass in the field of mental pathology to find human examples whose declarations perplex us: they are most certainly false, but we are unable to detect whether the subject does or does not know he is lying. Supposing, absurdly, that the liar should for one instant become truthful, he himself would not know how to answer the dilemma; in the act of lying he is an actor totally fused with his part, no longer distinguishable from it. A glaring example of this during the days in which I am writing is the behavior in court of the Turk Ali Agca, the would-be assassin of Pope John-Paul II.

The best way to defend oneself against the invasion of burdensome memories is to impede their entry, to extend a *cordon sanitaire*. It is easier to deny entry to a memory than to free oneself from it after it has been recorded. This, in substance, was the purpose of many of the artifices thought up by the Nazi commanders in order to protect the consciences of those assigned to do the dirty work and to ensure their services, disagreeable even for the most hardened cutthroats. The *Einsatzkommandos*, who behind the front lines in Russia machine-gunned civilians beside common graves which the victims themselves had been forced to dig, were given all the liquor they wanted so that the massacre would be blurred by drunkenness. The well-known euphemisms ("final solution," "special treatment," the very term *Einsatzkommando*, literally, "prompt-employment unit," disguised a frightful reality) were not only used to deceive the victims and prevent defensive reactions on their part: they were also meant, within the limits of the possible, to prevent public opinion, and those sections of the army not directly involved, from finding out what was happening in all the territories occupied by the Third Reich.

At any rate, the entire history of the brief "millennial Reich" can be reread as a war against memory, an Orwellian falsification of memory, falsification of reality, negation of reality. All of Hitler's biographies, while disagreeing on the interpretation to be given to the life of this man so difficult to classify, agree on the flight from reality which marked his last years, especially beginning with the first Russian winter. He had forbidden and denied his subjects any access to truth, contaminating their morality and their memory; but, to a degree which gradually increased and attained complete paranoia in the Bunker, he barred the path of truth to himself as well. Like all gamblers, he erected around himself a stage set woven of superstitious lies and in which he ended by believing with the same fanatical faith that he demanded from every German. His collapse was not only a salvation for mankind but also a demonstration of the price to be paid when one dismembers the truth.

Also in the certainly much vaster field of the victim one observes a drifting of memory, but here, evidently, fraud is not involved. Anyone who suffers an injustice or an injury does not need to elaborate lies to exculpate himself of a guilt he does not have (even though, due to a paradoxical mechanism of which we shall speak, he may well feel ashamed of it); but this does not exclude the fact that his memories may also be altered. It has been noticed, for instance, that many survivors of wars or other complex and traumatic experiences tend unconsciously to filter their memory: summoning them up among themselves, or telling them to third persons, they prefer to dwell on moments of respite, on grotesque, strange, or relaxed intermezzos, and to skim over the most painful episodes, which are not called up willingly from the reservoir of memory and therefore with time tend to mist over, to lose their contours. The behavior of Count Ugolino is psychologically credible when he becomes reticent about telling Dante of his terrible death; he agrees to do so not out of acquiescence but only out of a feeling of posthumous revenge against his eternal enemy.

When we say, "I will never forget that," referring to some event which has profoundly wounded us but has not left in us or around us a material trace or a permanent void, we are foolhardy: in "civilian" life we gladly forget the details of a serious illness from which we have recovered, or those of a successful surgical operation.

For purposes of defense, reality can be distorted not only in memory but in the very act of taking place. Throughout the year of my imprisonment in Auschwitz I had Alberto D. as a fraternal friend: he was a robust, courageous young man, more clearsighted than the average and therefore very critical of the many who fabricated for themselves, and reciprocally administered to each other, consolatory illusions ("The war will be over in two weeks," "There will be no more selections," "The English have landed in Greece," "The Polish Partisans are about to liberate the camp," and so on, rumors heard nearly every day and punctually given the lie by reality). Alberto had been deported together with his forty-five-year-old father. In the imminence of the great selection of October 1944, Alberto and I had commented on this event with fright, impotent rage, rebellion, resignation, but without seeking refuge in comforting truths. The selection came, Alberto's "old" father was chosen for the gas, and in the space of a few hours Alberto changed. He had heard rumors that seemed to him worthy of belief: the Russians are close by, the Germans would no longer dare persist in the slaughter, that was not a selection like the others, it was not for the gas chamber, but had been made to choose the weakened but salvageable prisoners, in fact like his father, who was very tired but not ill; indeed, he even knew where they would be sent, to Jaworzno, not far away, to a special camp for convalescents fit only for light labor.

Naturally his father was never seen again and Alberto

himself vanished during the evacuation march from the camp, in January 1945. Strangely, without knowing about Alberto's behavior, his relatives who had remained hidden in Italy, escaping capture, behaved in the same way, rejecting an unendurable truth, constructing a different one for themselves. As soon as I was repatriated, I considered it my duty to go immediately to Alberto's hometown to tell his mother and his brother what I knew. I was welcomed with courteous affection, but as soon as I began my story the mother begged me to stop: she already knew everything, at least as far as Alberto was concerned, and there was no point in my repeating the usual horror stories to her. She *knew* that her son, he alone, had been able to slip away from the column without being shot by the SS. He had hidden in the forest and was safe in Russian hands; he had not yet been able to send any word, but he would do so soon, she was certain of it; and now, would I please change the subject and tell her how I myself had survived. A year later I was by chance passing through that same town, and I again visited the family. The truth was slightly changed: Alberto was in a Soviet clinic, he was fine; but he had lost his memory, he no longer even remembered his name; he was improving though and would soon return—she had this from a reliable source.

Alberto never returned. More than forty years have passed. I did not have the courage to show up again and to counterpose my painful truth to the consolatory "truth" that, one helping the other, Alberto's relatives had fashioned for themselves.

An apology is in order. This very book is drenched in memory; what's more, a distant memory. Thus it draws from a suspect source and must be protected against itself.

So here then: it contains more considerations than memories, lingers more willingly on the state of affairs such as it is now than on the retroactive chronicle. Furthermore, the data it contains are strongly substantiated by the imposing literature that has been formed around the theme of the man submerged (or "saved"), also through the collaboration, voluntary or not, of the culprits of that time; and in this corpus the concordances are abundant, the discordances negligible. As for my personal memories, and the few unpublished anecdotes I have mentioned and will mention, I have diligently examined all of them: time has somewhat faded them, but they are in good consonance with their background and seem to me unaffected by the drifting I have described.

2

THE GRAY ZONE

AVE we—we who have returned—been able to understand and make others understand our experience? What we commonly mean by "understand" coincides with "simplify": without a profound simplification the world around us would be an infinite, undefined tangle that would defy our ability to orient ourselves and decide upon our actions. In short, we are compelled to reduce the knowable to a schema: with this purpose in view we have built for ourselves admirable tools in the course of evolution, tools which are the specific property of the human species—language and conceptual thought.

We also tend to simplify history; but the pattern within which events are ordered is not always identifiable in a single, unequivocal fashion, and therefore different historians may understand and construe history in ways that are incompatible with one another. Nevertheless, perhaps for reasons that go back to our origins as social animals, the need to divide the field into "we" and "they" is so strong that this pattern, this bipartition—friend/enemy—prevails over all others. Popular history, and also the history taught in schools, is influenced by this Manichaean tendency, which shuns half-tints and complexities: it is prone to reduce the river of human occurrences to conflicts, and the conflicts to duels—we and they, Athenians and Spartans, Romans and Carthaginians. This is certainly the reason for the enormous popularity of spectator sports, such as soccer, baseball, and boxing: the contenders are two teams or two individuals, clearly distinct and identifiable, and at the end of the match there are vanquished and victors. If the result is a draw, the spectator feels defrauded and disappointed. At the more or less unconscious level, he wanted winners and losers, which he identified with the good guys and the bad guys, respectively, because the good must prevail, otherwise the world would be subverted.

This *desire* for simplification is justified, but the same does not always apply to simplification itself, which is a working hypothesis, useful as long as it is recognized as such and not mistaken for reality. The greater part of historical and natural phenomena are not simple, or not simple in the way that we would like. Now, the network of human relationships inside the Lagers was not simple: it could not be reduced to the two blocs of victims and persecutors. Anyone who today reads (or writes) the history of the Lager reveals the tendency, indeed the need, to separate evil from good, to be able to take sides, to emulate Christ's gesture on Judgment Day: here the righteous, over there the reprobates. The young above all demand clarity, a sharp cut; their experience of the world being meager, they do not like ambiguity. In any case, their expectation reproduces exactly that of the newcomers to the Lagers, whether young or not; all of them, with the exception of those who had already gone through an analogous experience, expected to find a terrible but decipherable world, in conformity with that simple model which we atavistically carry within us—"we" inside and the enemy outside, separated by a sharply defined geographic frontier.

Instead, the arrival in the Lager was indeed a shock because of the surprise it entailed. The world into which one was precipitated was terrible, yes, but also indecipherable: it did not conform to any model; the enemy was all around but also inside, the "we" lost its limits, the contenders were not two, one could not discern a single frontier but rather many confused, perhaps innumerable frontiers, which stretched between each of us. One entered hoping at least for the solidarity of one's companions in misfortune, but the hoped for allies, except in special cases, were not there; there were instead a thousand sealed off monads, and between them a desperate covert and continuous struggle. This brusque revelation, which became manifest from the very first hours of imprisonment, often in the instant form of a concentric aggression on the part of those in whom one hoped to find future allies, was so harsh as to cause the immediate collapse of one's capacity to resist. For many it was lethal, indirectly or even directly: it is difficult to defend oneself against a blow for which one is not prepared.

Various aspects can be identified in this aggression. Remember that the concentration camp system even from its origins (which coincide with the rise to power of Nazism in Germany) had as its primary purpose shattering the adversaries' capacity to resist: for the camp management the new arrival was by definition an adversary, whatever the label attached to him might be, and he must immediately be demolished to make sure that he did not become an example or a germ of organized resistance. On this point the SS had very clear ideas, and it is from this viewpoint that the entire sinister ritual must be interpreted—varying from Lager to Lager, but basically similar—which accompanied the arrival: kicks and punches right away, often in the face; an orgy of orders screamed with true or simulated rage; complete nakedness after being stripped; the shaving off of all one's hair; the outfitting in rags. It is difficult to say whether all these details were devised by some expert or methodically perfected on the basis of experience, but they certainly were willed and not casual: it was all staged, as was quite obvious.

Nevertheless, the entry ritual, and the moral collapse it promoted, was abetted more or less consciously by the other components of the concentration camp world: the simple prisoners and the privileged ones. Rarely was a newcomer received, I won't say as a friend but at least as a companion-in-misfortune; in the majority of cases, those with seniority (and seniority was acquired in three or four months; the changeover was swift!) showed irritation or even hostility. The "newcomer" (*Zugang:* one should note that in German this is an abstract, administrative term, meaning "access," "entry") was envied because he still seemed to have on him the smell of home, and it was an absurd envy, because in fact one suffered much more during the first days of imprisonment than later on, when habituation on one hand and experience on the other made it possible to construct oneself a shelter. He was derided and subjected to cruel pranks, as happens in all communities with "conscripts" and "rookies," as well as in the initiation ceremonies of primitive peoples: and there is no doubt that life in the Lager involved a regression, leading back precisely to primitive behavior.

It is probable that the hostility toward the *Zugang* was in substance motivated like all other forms of intolerance, that is, it consisted in an unconscious attempt to consolidate the "we" at the expense of the "they," to create, in short, that solidarity among the oppressed whose absence was the source of additional suffering, even though not perceived openly. Vying for prestige also came into play, a seemingly irrepressible need in our civilization: the despised crowd of seniors was prone to recognize in the new arrival a target on which to vent its humiliation, to find compensation at his expense, to build for itself and at his expense a figure of a lower rank on whom to discharge the burden of the offenses received from above.

As for the privileged prisoners, the situation was more complex, and also more important: in my opinion, it is in fact fundamental. It is naive, absurd, and historically false to believe that an infernal system such as National Socialism sanctifies its victims: on the contrary, it degrades them, it makes them resemble itself, and this all the more when they are available, blank, and lacking a political or moral armature. From many signs it would seem the time has come to explore the space which separates (and not only in Nazi Lagers) the victims from the persecutors, and to do so with a lighter hand, and with a less turbid spirit than has been done, for instance, in a number of films. Only a schematic rhetoric can claim that that space is empty: it never is, it is studded with obscene or pathetic figures (sometimes they possess both qualities simultaneously) whom it is indispensable to know if we want to know the human species, if we want to know how to defend our souls when a similar test should once more loom before us, or even if we only want to understand what takes place in a big industrial factory.

Privileged prisoners were a minority within the Lager population; nevertheless they represent a potent majority among survivors. In fact, even apart from the hard labor, the beatings, the cold, and the illnesses, the food ration was decisively insufficient for even the most frugal prisoner: the physiological reserves of the organism were consumed in two or three months, and death by hunger, or by diseases induced by hunger, was the prisoner's normal destiny, avoidable only with additional food. Obtaining that extra nourishment required a privilege—large or small, granted or conquered, astute or violent, licit or illicit—whatever it took to lift oneself above the norm.

Now, one mustn't forget that the greater part of the memories, spoken or written, of those who came back begin with the collision with the concentrationary reality and, simultaneously, the unforeseen and uncomprehended aggression on the part of a new and strange enemy, the functionary-prisoner, who instead of taking you by the hand, reassuring you, teaching you the way, throws himself at you, screaming in a language you do not understand, and strikes you in the face. He wants to tame you, extinguish any spark of dignity that he has lost and you perhaps still preserve. But trouble is in store for you if this dignity drives you to react. There is an unwritten but iron law, *Zurüchschlagen:* answering blows with blows is an intolerable transgression that can only occur to the mind of a "newcomer," and anyone who commits it must be made an example. Other functionaries rush to the defense of the threatened order, and the culprit is beaten with rage and method until he's tamed or dead. Privilege, by definition, defends and protects privilege.

I remember now that the local Yiddish and Polish term to indicate privilege was *protekcja*, pronounced "protektsia," and is of obvious Italian and Latin origin. I was told the story of an Italian "newcomer," a Partisan, flung into a work Lager with the label "political prisoner" when he still had his full strength. He had been beaten when the soup was being distributed and he had dared to shove the distributor-functionary: the latter's colleagues rushed to his aid, and the culprit was made an example of by being drowned, his head held down in the soup tub.

The ascent of the privileged, not only in the Lager but in all human coexistence, is an anguishing but unfailing phenomenon: only in utopias is it absent. It is the duty of righteous men to make war on all undeserved privilege, but one must not forget that this is a war without end. Where power is exercised by few or only one against the many, privilege is born and proliferates, even against the will of the power itself. On the other hand, it is normal for power to tolerate and encourage privilege. Let us confine ourselves to the Lager, which (even in its Soviet version) can be considered an excellent "laboratory": the hybrid class of the prisoner-functionary constitutes its armature and at the same time its most disquieting feature. It is a gray zone, poorly defined, where the two camps of masters and servants both diverge and converge. This gray zone possesses an incredibly complicated internal structure and contains within itself enough to confuse our need to judge.

The gray zone of *protekcja* and collaboration springs from multiple roots. In the first place, the more the sphere of power is restricted, the more it needs external auxiliaries. The Nazism of the final years could not do without these external auxiliaries, determined as it was to maintain its order within subjugated Europe and feed the front lines of the war, bled white by their opponents' growing military resistance. The occupied countries had to provide not only labor but also forces of order, delegates and administrators of the German power, which was by now committed elsewhere to the point of exhaustion. Within this category fall, albeit to varying degrees, Quisling in Norway, the Vichy government in France, the Judenrat in Warsaw, the Salò Republic in Italy, right down to the Ukrainian and Baltic mercenaries employed elsewhere for the filthiest tasks (never in combat) and the *Sonderkommandos,* about which we will have more to say.

But collaborators who originate in the adversary camp, ex-enemies, are untrustworthy by definition: they betrayed once and they can betray again. It is not enough to relegate them to marginal tasks; the best way to bind them is to burden them with guilt, cover them with blood, compromise them as much as possible, thus establishing a bond of complicity so that they can no longer turn back. This way of proceeding has been well known to criminal associations of all times and places. The Mafia has always practiced it. It is also the only way to explain the otherwise indecipherable excesses of Italian terrorism in the 1970s.

In the second place, and in contrast to a certain hagiographic and rhetorical stylization, the harsher the oppression, the more widespread among the oppressed is the willingness, with all its infinite nuances and motivations, to collaborate: terror, ideological seduction, servile imitation of the victor, myopic desire for any power whatsoever, even though ridiculously circumscribed in space and time, cowardice, and, finally, lucid calculation aimed at eluding the imposed orders and order. All these motives, singly or combined, have come into play in the creation of this gray zone, whose components are bonded together by the wish to preserve and consolidate established privilege vis-à-vis those without privilege.

Before discussing separately the motives that impelled some prisoners to collaborate to some extent with the Lager authorities, however, it is necessary to declare the imprudence of issuing hasty moral judgment on such human cases. Certainly, the greatest responsibility lies with the system, the very structure of the totalitarian state; the concurrent guilt on the part of individual big and small collaborators (never likable, never transparent!) is always difficult to evaluate. It is a judgment that we would like to entrust only to those who found themselves in similar circumstances and had the opportunity to test for themselves what it means to act in a state of coercion. Alessandro Manzoni, the nine-teenth-century novelist and poet knew this quite well: "Provocateurs, oppressors, all those who in some way in-jure others, are guilty, not only of the evil they commit, but also of the perversion into which they lead the spirit of the offended." The condition of the offended does not exclude culpability, which is often objectively serious, but I know of no human tribunal to which one could delegate the judg-ment.

If it were up to me, if I were forced to judge, I would lightheartedly absolve all those whose concurrence in the guilt was minimal and for whom coercion was of the high-est degree. Around us, prisoners without rank, swarmed low-ranking functionaries, a picturesque fauna: sweepers, kettle washers, night watchmen, bed smoothers (who ex-ploited to their minuscule advantage the German fixation about bunks made up flat and square), checkers of lice and scabies, messengers, interpreters, assistants' assistants. In general, they were poor devils like ourselves, who worked full time like everyone else but who for an extra half-liter of soup were willing to carry out these and other "tertiary" functions: innocuous, sometimes useful, often invented out of the whole cloth. They were rarely violent, but they tended to develop a typically corporate mentality and ener-getically defended their "job" against anyone from below or above who might covet it. Their privilege, which at any rate entailed supplementary hardships and efforts, gained them very little and did not spare them from the discipline and suffering of everyone else; their hope for life was substantially the same as that of the unprivileged. They were coarse and arrogant, but they were not regarded as enemies.

Judgment becomes more tentative and varied for those who occupied commanding positions: the chiefs (*Kapos*: the German term derives directly from the Italian *capo*, and the truncated pronunciation, introduced by the French prisoners, spread only many years later, popularized by Pontecorvo's movie of the same name and preferred in Italy precisely because of its differentiating value) of the labor squads, the barracks chiefs, the clerks, all the way to the world (whose existence at that time I did not even suspect) of the prisoners who performed diverse, at times most delicate duties in the camps' administrative offices, the Political Section (actually a section of the Gestapo), the Labor Service, and the punishment cells. Some of these, thanks to skill or luck, had access to the most secret information of the respective Lagers and, like Herman Langbein in Auschwitz, Eugen Kogan in Buchenwald, and Hans Marsalek in Mauthausen, later became their historians. One does not know whether to admire more their personal courage or their cunning, which enabled them to help their companions in many concrete ways, by attentively studying the individual SS officers with whom they had contact and sensing who among them might be corrupted, who dissuaded from the crueler decisions, who blackmailed, who deceived, who frightened by the prospect of a *redde rationem* at the war's end. Some of them, the three mentioned, for example, were also members of secret defense organizations, and therefore the power they wielded thanks to their positions was counterbalanced by the extreme risk they ran, inasmuch as they were both "resistors" and the repositories of secrets.

The functionaries described were not at all, or were only apparently, collaborators, but on the contrary camouflaged opponents. Not so the greater part of the other persons with positions of command, human specimens who ranged from the mediocre to the execrable. Rather than wearing one down, power corrupts; all the more intensely did their power corrupt, since it had a peculiar nature.

Power exists in all the varieties of the human social organization, more or less controlled, usurped, conferred from above or recognized from below, assigned by merit, corporate solidarity, blood, or position. Probably a certain degree of man's domination over man is inscribed in our genetic patrimony as gregarious animals. There is no proof that power is intrinsically harmful to the collectivity. But the power of which the functionaries of whom we are speaking disposed, even if they were low-ranking, such as the *Kapos* of the work squads, was, in substance, unlimited; or, more accurately put, a lower limit was imposed on their violence, in the sense that they were punished or deposed if they did not prove to be sufficiently harsh, but there was no upper limit. In other words, they were free to commit the worst atrocities on their subjects as punishment for any transgressions, or even without any motive whatsoever: until the end of 1943 it was not unusual for a prisoner to be beaten to death by a *Kapo* without the latter having to fear any sanctions. Only later on, when the need for labor became more acute, were a number of limitations introduced: the mistreatment the *Kapos* were allowed to inflict on the prisoners could not permanently diminish their working ability. But by then the malpractice was established and the regulation was not always respected.

Thus the Lager, on a smaller scale but with amplified characteristics, reproduced the hierarchical structure of the totalitarian state, in which all power is invested from above and control from below is almost impossible. But this "almost" is important: never has there existed a state that was really "totalitarian" from this point of view. Never has some form of reaction, a corrective of the total tyranny, been lacking, not even in the Third Reich or Stalin's Soviet Union: in both cases public opinion, the magistrature, the foreign press, the churches, the feeling for justice and humanity that ten or twenty years of tyranny were not enough to eradicate, have to a greater or lesser extent acted as a brake. Only in the Lager was the restraint from below nonexistent and the power of these small satraps absolute. It is understandable that power of such magnitude overwhelmingly attracted the human type who is greedy for power, that even individuals with moderate instincts aspired to it, seduced by the many material advantages of the position, and that the latter became fatally intoxicated by the power at their disposal.

Who became a *Kapo?* It is once again necessary to distinguish. The first to be offered this possibility, that is, those individuals in whom the Lager commander or his delegates (who were often good psychologists) discerned a potential collaborator, were the common criminals, taken from prisons, to whom a career as a torturer offered an excellent alternative to detention. Then came political prisoners broken by five or ten years of sufferings, or in any case morally debilitated. Later on it was Jews who saw in the particle of authority being offered them the only possible escape from the "final solution." But many, as we mentioned, spontaneously aspired to power, sadists, for example, certainly not numerous but very much feared, because for them the position of privilege coincided with the possibility of inflicting suffering and humiliation on those below them. The frustrated sought power as well, and this too is a feature in which the microcosm of the Lager reproduced the macrocosm of totalitarian society: in both, without regard to ability and merit, power was generously granted to those willing to pay homage to hierarchic authority, thus attaining an otherwise unattainable social elevation. Finally, power was sought by the many among the oppressed who had been contaminated by their oppressors and unconsciously strove to identify with them.

This mimesis, this identification or imitation, or exchange of roles between oppressor and victim, has provoked much discussion. True and invented, disturbing and banal, acute and stupid things have been said: it is not virgin terrain; on the contrary it is a badly plowed field, trampled and torn up. The film director Liliana Cavani, who was asked to express briefly the meaning of a beautiful and false film of hers, declared: "We are all victims or murderers, and we accept these roles voluntarily. Only Sade and Dostoevsky have really understood this." She also said she believed "that in every environment, in every relationship, there is a victim-executioner dynamism more or less clearly expressed and generally lived on an unconscious level."

I am not an expert on the unconscious and the mind's depths, but I do know that few people are experts in this sphere and that these few are the most cautious. I do not know, and it does not much interest me to know, whether in my depths there lurks a murderer, but I do know that I was a guiltless victim and I was not a murderer. I know that the murderers existed, not only in Germany, and still exist, retired or on active duty, and that to confuse them with their victims is a moral disease or an aesthetic affectation or a sinister sign of complicity; above all, it is precious service rendered (intentionally or not) to the negators of truth. I know that in the Lager, and more generally on the human stage, everything happens, and that therefore the single example proves little. Having said all this quite clearly, and reaffirmed that confusing the two roles means wanting to becloud our need for justice at its foundation, I should make a few more remarks.

It remains true that in the Lager, and outside, there exist gray, ambiguous persons, ready to compromise. The extreme pressure of the Lager tends to increase their ranks; they are the rightful owners of a quota of guilt (which grows apace with their freedom of choice), and besides this they are the vectors and instruments of the system's guilt. It remains true that the majority of the oppressors, during or (more often) after their deeds, realized that what they were doing or had done was iniquitous, or perhaps experienced doubts or discomfort, or were even punished, but this suffering is not enough to enroll them among the victims. By the same token, the prisoners' errors and weaknesses are not enough to rank them with their custodians: the prisoners of the Lagers, hundreds of thousands of persons of all social classes, from almost all the countries of Europe, represented an average, unselected sample of humanity. Even if one did not want to take into account the infernal environment into which they had been abruptly flung, it is illogical to demand—and rhetorical and false to maintain—that they all and always followed the behavior expected of saints and stoic philosophers. In reality, in the vast majority of cases, their behavior was rigidly preordained. In the space of a few weeks or months the deprivations to which they were subjected led them to a condition of pure survival, a daily struggle against hunger, cold, fatigue, and blows in which the room for choices (especially moral choices) was reduced to zero. Among these, very few survived the test, and this thanks to the conjunction of many improbable events. In short, they were saved by luck, and there is not much sense in trying to find something common to all their destinies, beyond perhaps their initial good health.

An extreme case of collaboration is represented by the *Sonderkommandos* of Auschwitz and the other extermination camps. Here one hesitates to speak of privilege: whoever belonged to this group was privileged only to the extent that—but at what cost!—he had enough to eat for a few months, certainly not because he could be envied. With this duly vague definition, "Special Squad," the SS referred to the group of prisoners entrusted with running the crematoria. It was their task to maintain order among the new arrivals (often completely unaware of the destiny awaiting them) who were to be sent into the gas chambers, to extract the corpses from the chambers, to pull gold teeth from jaws, to cut women's hair, to sort and classify clothes, shoes, and the contents of the luggage, to transport the bodies to the crematoria and oversee the operation of the ovens, to extract and eliminate the ashes. The Special Squad in Auschwitz numbered, depending on the moment, from seven hundred to one thousand active members.

These Special Squads did not escape everyone else's fate. On the contrary, the SS exerted the greatest diligence to prevent any man who had been part of it from surviving and telling. Twelve squads succeeded each other in Auschwitz, each remaining operative for a few months, whereupon it was suppressed, each time with a different trick to head off possible resistance. As its initiation, the next squad burnt the corpses of its predecessors. In October 1944 the last squad rebelled against the SS, blew up one of the crematoria, and was exterminated in an unequal battle that I will discuss later on. The survivors of the Special Squad were therefore very few, having escaped death because of some unforeseeable whim of fate. None of them, after the Liberation, has spoken willingly, and no one speaks willingly about their frightful condition. The information we have about these squads comes from the meager depositions of survivors, from the admissions of their "instigators" tried in various courts, from hints contained in the depositions of German or Polish "civilians" who by chance came into contact with the squads, and lastly, from diary pages written feverishly for future memory and buried with extreme care near the crematoria in Auschwitz by some of the squads' members. All these sources are in agreement, and yet we have found it difficult, almost impossible, to form an image for ourselves of how these men lived day by day, saw themselves, accepted their condition.

At first, the SS chose them from among the prisoners already registered in the Lager, and it has been testified that the choice was made not only on the basis of physical strength but also by a deep study of physiognomies. In a few rare cases enrollment took place as a punishment. Later on it was considered preferable to pick out the candidates directly at the railroad platform, on the arrival of each convoy: the SS "psychologists" noticed that recruitment was easier if one drew them from among those desperate, disoriented people, exhausted from the journey, bereft of resistance, at the crucial moment of stepping off the train, when every new arrival truly felt on the threshold of the darkness and terror of an unearthly space.

The Special Squads were made up largely of Jews. In a certain sense this is not surprising since the Lager's main purpose was to destroy Jews, and, beginning in 1943, the Auschwitz population was 90–95 percent Jews. From another point of view, one is stunned by this paroxysm of perfidy and hatred: it must be the Jews who put the Jews into the ovens; it must be shown that the Jews, the subrace, the submen, bow to any and all humiliation, even to destroying themselves. On the other hand, we know that not all the SS gladly accepted massacre as a daily task; delegating part of the work—and indeed the filthiest part—to the victims themselves was meant to (and probably did) ease a few consciences here and there.

Obviously it would be iniquitous to attribute such acquiescence to some specifically Jewish peculiarity: members of the Special Squads were also non-Jewish, German and Polish prisoners, although with the "more dignified" duties of *Kapos*, and also Russian prisoners of war, whom the Nazis considered only one degree superior to the Jews. They were few, because the Russians in Auschwitz were few (for the greater part having been exterminated before, immediately after capture, machine-gunned at the edge of enormous common graves): but they did not behave any differently from the Jews.

The Special Squads, being bearers of a horrendous secret, were kept rigorously apart from the other prisoners and the outside world. Nevertheless, as anyone who has gone through similar experiences knows, no barrier is ever without a flaw: information, possibly incomplete or distorted, has a tremendous power of penetration, and some of it always does filter through. Concerning these squads, vague and mangled rumors already circulated among us during our imprisonment and were confirmed afterward by the other sources mentioned before. But the intrinsic horror of this human condition has imposed a sort of reserve on all the testimony, so that even today it is difficult to conjure up an image of "what it meant" to be forced to exercise this trade for months. It has been testified that a large amount of alcohol was put at the disposal of those wretches and that they were in a permanent state of complete debasement and prostration. One of them declared: "Doing this work, one either goes crazy the first day or gets accustomed to it." Another, though: "Certainly, I could have killed myself or got myself killed; but I wanted to survive, to avenge myself and bear witness. You mustn't think that we are monsters; we are the same as you, only much more unhappy."

Clearly what we know they said, and the innumerable other things they probably said but did not reach us, cannot be taken literally. One cannot expect from men who have known such extreme destitution a deposition in the juridical sense, but something that is at once a lament, a curse, an expiation, an attempt to justify and rehabilitate oneself: a liberating outburst rather than a Medusa-faced truth.

Conceiving and organizing the squads was National Socialism's most demonic crime. Behind the pragmatic aspect (to economize on able men, to impose on others the most atrocious tasks) other more subtle aspects can be perceived. This institution represented an attempt to shift onto others—specifically, the victims—the burden of guilt, so that they were deprived of even the solace of innocence. It is neither easy nor agreeable to dredge this abyss of viciousness, and yet I think it must be done, because what could be perpetrated yesterday could be attempted again tomorrow, could overwhelm us and our children. One is tempted to turn away with a grimace and close one's mind: this is a temptation one must resist. In fact, the existence of the squads had a meaning, a message: "We, the master race, are your destroyers, but you are no better than we are; if we so wish, and we do so wish, we can destroy not only your bodies but also your souls, just as we have destroyed ours."

Miklos Nyiszli, a Hungarian physician, was one of the very few survivors of the last Special Squad in Auschwitz. He was a renowned anatomical pathologist, expert in autopsies and the chief doctor of the Birkenau SS whose services Mengele—who died a few years ago, escaping justice—had secured; he had given him special treatment and considered him almost a colleague. Nyiszli was supposed to devote himself in particular to the study of twins: in fact, Birkenau was the only place in the world where it was possible to study the corpses of twins killed at the same moment. Alongside this particular task of his, to which, it should be said in passing, it does not appear he strenuously objected, Nyiszli was also the attending physician of the squad, with which he lived in close contact. Well, he recounts an episode that seems significant to me.

The SS, as I already said, carefully chose, from the Lagers or the arriving convoys, the candidates for the squads, and did not hesitate to eliminate on the spot anyone who refused or seemed unsuitable for those duties. The SS treated the newly engaged members with the same contempt and detachment that they were accustomed to show toward all prisoners and Jews in particular. It had been inculcated in them that these were despicable beings, enemies of Germany, and therefore not entitled to life; in the most favorable instance, they should be compelled to work until they died of exhaustion. But this is not how they behaved with the veterans of the squad: in them, they recognized to some extent colleagues, by now as inhuman as themselves, hitched to the same cart, bound together by the foul link of imposed complicity. So, Nyiszli tells how during a "work" pause he attended a soccer game between the SS and the SK (*Sonderkommando*), that is to say, between a group representing the SS on guard at the crematorium and a group representing the Special Squad. Other men of the SS and the rest of the squad are present at the game; they take sides, bet, applaud, urge the players on as if, rather than at the gates of hell, the game were taking place on the village green.

Nothing of this kind ever took place, nor would it have been conceivable, with other categories of prisoners; but with them, with the "crematorium ravens," the SS could enter the field on an equal footing, or almost. Behind this armistice one hears satanic laughter: it is consummated, we have succeeded, you no longer are the other race, the anti-race, the prime enemy of the millennial Reich; you are no longer the people who reject idols. We have embraced you, corrupted you, dragged you to the bottom with us. You are like us, you proud people: dirtied with your own blood, as we are. You too, like us and like Cain, have killed the brother. Come, we can play together.

Nyiszli describes another episode that deserves consideration. In the gas chamber have been jammed together and murdered the components of a recently arrived convoy, and the squad is performing its horrendous everyday work, sorting out the tangle of corpses, washing them with hoses, and transporting them to the crematorium, but on the floor they find a young woman who is still alive. The event is exceptional, unique; perhaps the human bodies formed a barrier around her, sequestered a pocket of air that remained breathable. The men are perplexed. Death is their trade at all hours, death is a habit because, precisely, "one either goes mad on the first day or becomes accustomed to it," but this woman is alive. They hide her, warm her, bring her beef broth, question her: the girl is sixteen years old, she cannot orient herself in space or time, does not know where she is, has gone through without understanding it the sequence of the sealed train, the brutal preliminary selection, the stripping, the entry into the chamber from which no one had ever come out alive. She has not understood, but she has seen; therefore she must die, and the men of the squad know it just as they know that they too must die for the same reason. But these slaves debased by alcohol and the daily slaughter are transformed; they no longer have before them the anonymous mass, the flood of frightened, stunned people coming off the boxcars: they have a person.

Can one help but think of the "unusual respect" and the hesitation of the "foul Monatto"* when faced by the individual case, faced by the child Cecilia killed by the plague whom, in Manzoni's novel *The Betrothed*, the mother refused to let be flung on the cart together with the heaped up corpses? Occurrences like this astonish because they conflict with the image we have of man in harmony with himself, coherent, monolithic; and they should not astonish because that is not how man is. Compassion and brutality can coexist in the same individual and in the same moment, despite all logic; and for all that, compassion itself eludes logic. There is no proportion between the pity we feel and the extent of the pain by which the pity is aroused: a single Anne Frank excites more emotion than the myriads who suffered as she did but whose image has remained in the shadows. Perhaps it is necessary that it can be so. If we had to and were able to suffer the sufferings of everyone, we could not live. Perhaps the dreadful gift of pity for the

* The men employed to bury the dead during a plague.

many is granted only to saints; to the Monatti, to the members of the Special Squad, and to all of us there remains in the best of cases only the sporadic pity addressed to the single individual, the *Mitmensch*, the co-man: the human being of flesh and blood standing before us, within the reach of our providentially myopic senses.

A doctor is called, and he revives the girl with an injection: yes, the gas has not had its effect, she will survive, but where and how? Just then Muhsfeld, one of the SS men attached to the death installations, arrives. The doctor calls him to one side and presents the case to him. Muhsfeld hesitates, then he decides: No, the girl must die. If she were older, it would be a different matter, she would have more sense, perhaps she could be convinced to keep quiet about what has happened to her. But she's only sixteen: she can't be trusted. And yet, he does not kill her with his own hands. He calls one of his underlings to eliminate her with a blow to the nape of the neck. Now, this man Muhsfeld was not a compassionate person; his daily ration of slaughter was studded with arbitrary and capricious acts, marked by his inventions of refined cruelty. He was tried in 1947, sentenced to death and hung in Krakow and this was right, but not even he was a monolith. Had he lived in a different environment and epoch, he probably would have behaved like any other common man.

In *The Brothers Karamazov* Grushenka tells the fable of the little onion. A vicious old woman dies and goes to hell, but her guardian angel, straining his memory, recalls that she once, only once, gave a beggar the gift of a little onion she had dug up from her garden. He holds the little onion out to her, and the old woman grasps it and is lifted out of the flames of hell. This fable has always struck me as revolting: what human monster did not throughout his life make the gift of a little onion, if not to others, to his children, his wife, his dog? That single, immediately erased instant of pity is certainly not enough to absolve Muhsfeld. It is enough, however, to place him too, although at its extreme boundary, within the gray band, that zone of ambiguity which radiates out from regimes based on terror and obsequiousness.

It is not difficult to judge Muhsfeld, and I do not believe that the tribunal which sentenced him had any doubts. On the other hand, in contrast to this, our need and our ability to judge falters when confronted by the Special Squad. Questions immediately arise, convulsed questions for which one would be hard pressed to find an answer that reassures us about man's nature. Why did they accept that task? Why didn't they rebel? Why didn't they prefer death?

To a certain extent, the facts available to us permit us to attempt an answer. Not all did accept; some did rebel, knowing they would die. Concerning at least one case we have precise information: a group of four hundred Jews from Corfu, who in July 1944 had been included in the squad, refused without exception to do the work and were immediately gassed to death. We have learned of various individual mutinies, all immediately punished by an atrocious death (Filip Müller, one of the squads' very few survivors, tells of a companion whom the SS pushed into the oven alive), and many cases of suicide at the moment of recruitment, or immediately after. Finally, it must be remembered that it was the Special Squad which in October 1944 organized the only desperate attempt at revolt in the history of the Auschwitz Lager.

The information about this exploit that has come down to us is neither complete nor without contradictions. It is known that the insurgents (the personnel of two of the five

Auschwitz-Birkenau crematoria), poorly armed and without contacts with the Polish Partisans outside the Lager or the clandestine defense organization inside the Lager, blew up Crematorium no. 3 and engaged the SS in battle. The battle was soon over, and a number of the insurgents managed to cut the barbed wire and escape to the outside but were captured soon afterward. Not one of them survived: approximately four hundred and fifty were immediately killed by the SS; among the latter, three were killed and twelve wounded.

Those whom we know about, the miserable manual laborers of the slaughter, are therefore the others, those who from one shift to the next preferred a few more weeks of life (what a life) to immediate death, but who in no instance induced themselves, or were induced, to kill with their own hands. I repeat: I believe that no one is authorized to judge them, not those who lived through the experience of the Lager and even less those who did not. I would invite anyone who dares pass judgment to carry out upon himself, with sincerity, a conceptual experiment: Let him imagine, if he can, that he has lived for months or years in a ghetto, tormented by chronic hunger, fatigue, promiscuity, and humiliation; that he has seen die around him, one by one, his beloved; that he is cut off from the world, unable to receive or transmit news; that, finally, he is loaded onto a train, eighty or a hundred persons to a boxcar; that he travels into the unknown, blindly, for sleepless days and nights; and that he is at last flung inside the walls of an indecipherable inferno. This, it seems to me, is the true *Befehlnotstand*, the "state of compulsion following an order": not the one systematically and impudently invoked by the Nazis dragged to judgment and, later on (but in their footsteps), by the war criminals of many other countries. The former is a rigid either/or, immediate obedience or death; the latter is an internal fact at the center of power and could have been resolved (actually often was resolved) by some maneuver, some slowdown in career, moderate punishment, or, in the worst of cases, the objector's transfer to the front.

The experiment I have proposed is not pleasant. Vercors tried to describe it in his story *Les Armes de la nuit* (Albin Michel, Paris, 1953), in which he speaks of "the death of the soul," and which reread today seems to me intolerably infected by aestheticism and literary lechery. Undoubtedly, however, it deals with the death of the soul. Now nobody can know for how long and under what trials his soul can resist before yielding or breaking. Every human being possesses a reserve of strength whose extent is unknown to him, be it large, small, or nonexistent, and only through extreme adversity can we evaluate it. Even apart from the extreme case of the Special Squads, often those of us who have returned, when we describe our vicissitudes, hear in response: "In your place I would not have lasted for a single day." This statement does not have a precise meaning: one is never in another's place. Each individual is so complex that there is no point in trying to foresee his behavior, all the more so in extreme situations; nor is it possible to foresee one's own behavior. Therefore I ask that we meditate on the story of "the crematorium ravens" with pity and rigor, but that judgment of them be suspended.

The same *impotentia judicandi* paralyzes us when confronted by the Rumkowski case. The story of Chaim Rumkowski is not exactly a Lager story, although it reaches its conclusion in the Lager. It is a ghetto story, but so eloquent on the fundamental theme of human ambiguity fatally provoked by oppression that I would say it fits our discourse only too well. I repeat it here, even though I have already told it elsewhere.* On my return from Auschwitz I found in my pocket a curious coin of light alloy, which I have saved to this day. Scratched and corroded, on one side it has the Hebrew star (the "shield of David"), the date 1943, and the word *getto;* on the other side is the inscription *QUITTUNG ÜBER 10 MARK* and *DER ÄLTESTE DER JUDEN IN LITZMANNSTADT,* that is, respectively, *Receipt for ten marks* and *The elder of the Jews in Litzmannstadt.* In short, it was a coin for internal ghetto use. For many years I forgot about its existence, and then, around 1974, I was able to reconstruct its story, which is fascinating and sinister.

In honor of a certain General Litzmann, who had defeated the Russians during World War I, the Nazis had rechristened the Polish city of Lodz "Litzmannstadt." During the final months of 1944 the last survivors of the Lodz ghetto were deported to Auschwitz, and I probably found that now useless coin on the ground in the Lager.

In 1939 Lodz had seven hundred and fifty thousand inhabitants and was the most industrialized Polish city, the most "modern" and the ugliest: it made its living from the textile industry, like Manchester and Biella, and it was conditioned by the presence of a myriad of small and large factories, which were mostly antiquated even then. As in all cities of a certain importance in occupied Eastern Europe, the Nazis hastened to set up a ghetto in it, reinstating, aggravated by their modern ferocity, the regime of the medieval and Counter-Reformation ghettos. The Lodz ghetto, begun as early as February 1940, was first

* In *Moments of Reprieve* (New York: Summit Books, 1986).

chronologically and, after Warsaw's, second in number: it grew to more than one hundred and sixty thousand Jews and was disbanded only in the autumn of 1944. So it was the longest lived of the Nazi ghettos, and this must be attributed to two reasons: its economic importance and the perplexing personality of its president.

His name was Chaim Rumkowski. A failed minor industrialist, after varied travels and uneven fortunes he had settled in Lodz in 1917. In 1940 he was almost sixty and a widower without children. He enjoyed a certain esteem and was known as the director of Jewish charities and as an energetic, uncultivated, and authoritarian man. The position of president (or elder) of a ghetto was intrinsically frightful, but it was a position. It constituted social recognition, raised one a step up the ladder, and conferred rights and privileges, that is, authority—and Rumkowski passionately loved authority. How he happened to obtain the investiture is not known. Perhaps it was simply a hoax in the sinister Nazi style (Rumkowski was, or seemed to be, a fool with an air of respectability—in short, the ideal dupe); perhaps he himself had intrigued to be chosen, so strong in him must have been the will to power. The four years of his presidency, or, more precisely, his dictatorship, were an astonishing tangle of megalomaniac dream, barbaric vitality, and real diplomatic and organizational skill. He soon came to see himself in the role of absolute but enlightened monarch, and he was certainly encouraged along this path by his German masters, who, true enough, toyed with him, but appreciated his talents as a good administrator and man of order. He obtained from them the authorization to mint currency—both in metal (that coin of mine) and on watermarked paper that was officially supplied him—which was used to pay the exhausted workers in the ghetto. They could spend it in the ghetto stores to acquire their food rations, which on the average amounted to eight hundred calories a day (although at least two thousand are needed to survive in a condition of total repose).

From these famished citizens of his, Rumkowski aspired to obtain not only obedience and respect but also love: in this respect modern dictatorships differ from the ancient ones. Since he disposed of an army of excellent artists and craftsmen ready to perform at his slightest hint in exchange for a quarter loaf of bread, he gave orders to design and print stamps bearing his effigy, with his snow-white hair and beard haloed by the light of Hope and Faith. He had a carriage drawn by a skeleton nag in which he rode through the streets of his minuscule kingdom, streets crowded with beggars and postulants. He had a regal mantle and surrounded himself with a court of flatterers and henchmen; he had his courtier-poets compose hymns in which "his firm and powerful hands" were celebrated, as well as the peace and order which thanks to him reigned in the ghetto. He ordered that the children in the nefarious schools, devastated daily by epidemics, malnutrition, and German raids, should be assigned essays in praise "of our beloved and providential president." Like all autocrats, he hastened to organize an efficient police force, ostensibly to maintain order, but in fact to protect his own person and impose his discipline: six hundred guards armed with clubs, and an unspecified number of spies. He delivered many speeches, some of which have been preserved for us and whose style is unmistakable: he had adopted the oratorical technique of Mussolini and Hitler, the style of inspired recitation, the pseudo-colloquy with the crowd, the creation of consent through subjugation and plaudit. Perhaps this imitation of his was deliberate; perhaps instead it was unconscious identification with the model of the "necessary hero" who at the time dominated Europe and was sung by D'Annunzio. More likely, however, his attitude sprang from his condition as a small tyrant, impotent with those above him and omnipotent with those below him. He spoke like a man who has throne and scepter, who is not afraid of being contradicted or derided.

And yet his figure was more complex than it may appear thus far. Rumkowski was not only a renegade and an accomplice; to some extent, besides convincing others, he must have progressively convinced himself that he *was* a messiah, a savior of his people, whose welfare, at least at intervals, he must certainly have desired. One must benefit in order to feel beneficent, and feeling beneficent is gratifying even for a corrupt satrap. Paradoxically, his identification with the oppressor alternates, or goes hand in hand, with an identification with the oppressed, because, as Thomas Mann says, man is a mixed up creature. He becomes all the more confused, we might add, the more he is subjected to tensions: at that point he evades our judgment, just as a compass goes wild at the magnetic pole.

Even though he was constantly despised and derided by the Germans, Rumkowski probably thought of himself not as a servant but as a lord. He must have taken his own authority seriously: when the Gestapo, without warning, seized *his* councilmen, he came courageously to their rescue, exposing himself to jeers and slaps which he knew how to endure with dignity. On other occasions he tried to bargain with the Germans, who kept exacting more and more cloth from Lodz and from him ever more numerous contingents of useless mouths (children, old and sick people) to send to the gas chamber in Treblinka and, later on, Auschwitz. The very harshness with which he hastened

to repress signs of insubordination on the part of his subjects (there existed in Lodz, as in other ghettos, nuclei of
bold political resistance, with Zionist, Bundist, or Communist roots) did not originate so much in servility toward
the Germans, as in lese-majesty, indignation over the outrage inflicted on his regal person.

In September 1944, as the Russian front approached, the
Nazis initiated the liquidation of the Lodz ghetto. Men and
women by the tens of thousands were deported to Auschwitz, *anus mundi*, ultimate drainage site of the German
universe. Worn out as they were, they were all eliminated
almost immediately. About a thousand men remained in
the ghetto, to dismantle the machinery of the factories and
cancel the traces of the slaughter. They were liberated by
the Red Army shortly afterward, and it is to them that
we owe the information recorded here.

About Chaim Rumkowski's final fate two versions exist,
as though the ambiguity under whose sign he lived was
protracted to envelop his death. According to the first
version, in the course of the ghetto's liquidation he supposedly tried to oppose the deportation of his brother, from
whom he did not want to be separated, whereupon a German officer, it is said, proposed he should leave voluntarily
with his brother, and he is supposed to have accepted.
Another version claims instead that Rumkowski's rescue
was attempted by Hans Biebow, another figure drenched
in duplicity. This shady German industrialist was the functionary responsible for the ghetto's administration and at
the same time its exclusive contractor. Hence, his was
a delicate position, because the textile factories in Lodz
worked for the armed forces. Biebow was not a ferocious
beast. He was not interested in creating useless suffering
or punishing the Jews for the sin of being Jewish, but he

was interested in profiting from his contracts, in both legitimate and other ways. The torment in the ghetto touched
him, but only indirectly. He wanted the slave-workers to
work, and therefore he did not want them to die of hunger:
his moral sense ended there. In reality, he was the true
master of the ghetto, and he was linked to Rumkowski by
that buyer-supplier relationship which often becomes a
crude friendship. Biebow, a small jackal too cynical to take
race demonology seriously, would have liked to put off
forever the dismantling of the ghetto, which, for him, was
an excellent business deal, and to preserve Rumkowski, on
whose complicity he relied, from deportation. Here one
sees how often a realist is objectively better than a theoretician. But the theoreticians of the SS thought otherwise,
and they were the stronger. They were *grundlich* radicals:
get rid of the ghetto and get rid of Rumkowski.

Unable to deal with the matter otherwise, Biebow, who
had good connections, handed Rumkowski a letter addressed
to the Lager of his destination and guaranteed that it would
protect him and assure him special treatment. Rumkowski
supposedly asked for and obtained from Biebow the right to
travel to Auschwitz—he and his family—with the decorum
becoming his rank, that is, in a special car, attached to the
end of a convoy of freight cars packed with deportees without privileges. But there was only one fate for Jews in
German hands, whether they were cowards or heroes,
humble or proud. Neither the letter nor the special carriage
were able to save Chaim Rumkowski, the king of the Jews,
from the gas chamber.

A story like this is not self-contained. It is pregnant, full
of significance, asks more questions than it answers, sums
up in itself the entire theme of the gray zone and leaves

one dangling. It shouts and clamors to be understood, because in it one perceives a symbol, as in dreams and the signs of heaven.

Who was Rumkowski? Not a monster, nor a common man; yet many around us are like him. The failures that preceded his "career" are significant: few are the men who draw moral strength from failure. It seems to me that in his story it is possible to recognize in an exemplary form the almost physical necessity with which political coercion gives birth to that ill-defined sphere of ambiguity and compromise. At the foot of every absolute throne, men such as Rumkowski crowd in order to grab their small portion of power. It is a recurrent spectacle: we remember the deadly struggles during the last months of World War II in Hitler's court and among the ministers of Mussolini's Republic of Saló; they too gray men, blind first and criminal later, frenziedly dividing among themselves the shreds of an iniquitous and moribund authority. Power is like a drug: the need for either is unknown to anyone who has not tried them, but after the initiation, which (as for Rumkowski) can be fortuitous, the dependency and need for ever larger doses is born, as are the denial of reality and the return to childish dreams of omnipotence. If the interpretation of a Rumkowski intoxicated with power is valid, then the intoxication occurred not because of but rather despite the ghetto environment. In other words, the intoxication with power is so powerful as to prevail even under conditions seemingly designed to extinguish all individual will. In fact, in him as in his more famous models, the syndrome produced by protracted and undisputed power is clearly visible: a distorted view of the world, dogmatic arrogance, the need for adulation, convulsive clinging to the levers of command, and contempt for the law.

All this does not exonerate Rumkowski from his responsibilities. That a Rumkowski should have emerged from Lodz's affliction is painful and distressing. Had he survived his own tragedy, and the tragedy of the ghetto he contaminated, superimposing on it his histrionic image, no tribunal would have absolved him, nor, certainly, can we absolve him on the moral plane. But there are extenuating circumstances: an infernal order such as National Socialism exercises a frightful power of corruption, against which it is difficult to guard oneself. It degrades its victims and makes them similar to itself, because it needs both great and small complicities. To resist it requires a truly solid moral armature, and the one available to Chaim Rumkowski, the Lodz merchant, together with his entire generation, was fragile. But how strong is ours, the Europeans of today? How would each of us behave if driven by necessity and at the same time lured by seduction?

Rumkowski's story is the sorry, disquieting story of the *Kapos* and Lager functionaries, the small hierarchs who serve a regime to whose misdeeds they are willingly blind, the subordinates who sign everything because a signature costs little, those who shake their heads but acquiesce, those who say, "If I did not do it, someone else worse than I would."

Rumkowski, a symbolic and compendiary figure, must be placed in this band of half-consciences. Whether high or low it is difficult to say: only he could clarify this if he could speak before us, even lying, as he perhaps always lied, also to himself. He would in any case help us understand him, as every defendant helps his judge, even though he does not want to, even if he lies, because man's capacity to play a role is not unlimited.

But all this is not enough to explain the sense of urgency

and threat that emanates from this story. Perhaps its meaning is vaster: we are all mirrored in Rumkowski, his ambiguity is ours, it is our second nature, we hybrids molded from clay and spirit. His fever is ours, the fever of our Western civilization that "descends into hell with trumpets and drums," and its miserable adornments are the distorting image of our symbols of social prestige. His folly is that of presumptuous and mortal Man as he is described by Isabella in *Measure for Measure*, the Man who,

> Dressed in a little brief authority,
> Most ignorant of what he's most assured,
> His glassy essence, like an angry ape
> Plays such fantastic tricks before high heaven
> As makes the angels weep.

Like Rumkowski, we too are so dazzled by power and prestige as to forget our essential fragility. Willingly or not we come to terms with power, forgetting that we are all in the ghetto, that the ghetto is walled in, that outside the ghetto reign the lords of death, and that close by the train is waiting.

3
SHAME

A CERTAIN fixed image has been proposed innumerable times, consecrated by literature and poetry, and picked up by the cinema: "the quiet after the storm," when all hearts rejoice. "To be freed from pain / is delightful for us." The disease runs its course and health returns. To deliver us from imprisonment "our boys," the liberators, arrive just in time, with waving flags; the soldier returns and again finds his family and peace.

Judging by the stories told by many who came back and from my own memories, Leopardi the pessimist stretched the truth in this representation; despite himself, he showed himself to be an optimist. In the majority of cases, the hour of liberation was neither joyful nor lighthearted. For most it occurred against a tragic background of destruction, slaughter, and suffering. Just as they felt they were again becoming men, that is, responsible, the sorrows of men returned: the sorrow of the dispersed or lost family; the universal suffering all around; their own exhaustion, which seemed definitive, past cure; the problems of a life to begin all over again amid the rubble, often alone. Not "pleasure the son of misery," but misery the son of misery. Leaving pain behind was a delight for only a few fortunate beings, or only for a few instants, or for very simple souls; almost always it coincided with a phase of anguish.

Anguish is known to everyone, even children, and everyone knows that it is often blank, undifferentiated. Rarely does it carry a clearly written label that also contains its motivation; any label it does have is often mendacious. One can believe or declare oneself to be anguished for one reason and be so due to something totally different. One can think that one is suffering at facing the future and instead be suffering because of one's past; one can think that one is suffering for others, out of pity, out of compassion, and instead be suffering for one's own reasons, more or less profound, more or less avowable and avowed, sometimes so deep that only the specialist, the analyst of souls, knows how to exhume them.

Naturally, I dare not maintain that the movie script I referred to before is false in every case. Many liberations were experienced with full, authentic joy—above all by combatants, both military and political, who at that moment saw the aspirations of their militancy and their lives realized, and also on the part of those who had suffered less and for less time, or only in their own person and not because of their family, friends, or loved ones. And besides, luckily, human beings are not all the same: there are among us those who have the virtue and the privilege of extracting, isolating those instants of happiness, of enjoying them fully, as though they were extracting pure gold from dross. And finally, among the testimonies, written or spoken, some are unconsciously stylized, in which convention prevails over genuine memory: "Whoever is freed from slavery rejoices.

I too was liberated, hence I too rejoice over it. In all films, all novels, just as in *Fidelio*, the shattering of the chains is a moment of solemn or fervid jubilation, and so was mine." This is a specific case of that drifting of memory I mentioned in the first chapter, and which is accentuated with the passing of years and the piling up of the experiences of others, true or presumed, on one's own. But anyone who, purportedly or by temperament, shuns rhetoric, usually speaks in a different voice. This, for example, is how, on the last page of his memoir, *Eyewitness Auschwitz: Three Years in the Gas Chambers*, Filip Müller, whose experience was much more terrible than mine, describes his liberation:

> Although it may seem incredible, I had a complete letdown or depression. That moment, on which for three years all my thoughts and secret desires were concentrated, did not awaken happiness or any other feeling in me. I let myself fall from my pallet and crawled to the door. Once outside I tried vainly to go further, then I simply lay down on the ground in the woods and fell asleep.

I now reread the passage from my own book, *The Reawakening*, which was published in Italy only in 1963, although I had written these words as early as 1947. In it is a description of the first Russian soldiers facing our Lager packed with corpses and dying prisoners.

> They did not greet us, nor smile; they seemed oppressed, not only by pity but also by a confused restraint which sealed their mouths, and kept their eyes fastened on the funeral scene. It was the same shame which we knew so well, which submerged us after the selections, and every time we had to witness or undergo an outrage: the shame that the Germans never knew, the shame which the just

man experiences when confronted by a crime committed by another, and he feels remorse because of its existence, because of its having been irrevocably introduced into the world of existing things, and because his will has proven nonexistent or feeble and was incapable of putting up a good defense.

I do not think that there is anything I need erase or correct, but there is something I must add. That many (including me) experienced "shame," that is, a feeling of guilt during the imprisonment and afterward, is an ascertained fact confirmed by numerous testimonies. It may seem absurd, but it is a fact. I will try to interpret it myself and to comment on the interpretations of others.

As I mentioned at the start, the vague discomfort which accompanied liberation was not precisely shame, but it was perceived as such. Why? There are various possible explanations.

I will exclude certain exceptional cases: the prisoners who, almost all of them political, had the strength and opportunity to act within the Lager in defense of and to the advantage of their companions. We, the almost total majority of common prisoners, did not know about them and did not even suspect their existence, and logically so: due to obvious political and police necessity (the Political Section of Auschwitz was simply a branch of the Gestapo) they were forced to operate secretly, not only where the Germans were concerned but in regard to everyone. In Auschwitz, the concentrationary empire which in my time was constituted by 95 percent Jews, this political network was embryonic; I witnessed only one episode that should have led me to sense something had I not been crushed by the everyday travail.

Around May 1944 our almost innocuous *Kapo* was replaced, and the newcomer proved to be a fearsome individual. All *Kapos* gave beatings: this was an obvious part of their duties, their more or less accepted language. After all, it was the only language that everyone in that perpetual Babel could truly understand. In its various nuances it was understood as an incitement to work, a warning or punishment, and in the hierarchy of suffering it had a low rank. Now, the new *Kapo* gave his beatings in a different way, in a convulsive, malicious, perverse way: on the nose, the shin, the genitals. He beat to hurt, to cause suffering and humiliation. Not even, as with many others, out of blind racial hatred, but with the obvious intention of inflicting pain, indiscriminately, and without pretext, on all his subjects. Probably he was a mental case, but clearly under those conditions the indulgence that we today consider obligatory toward such sick people would have been out of place. I spoke about it with a colleague, a Jewish Croatian Communist: What should we do? How to protect ourselves? How to act collectively? He gave me a strange smile and simply said: "You'll see, he won't last long." In fact, the beater vanished within a week. But years later, during a meeting of survivors, I found out that some political prisoners attached to the Work Office inside the camp had the terrifying power of switching the registration numbers on the lists of prisoners destined to be gassed. Anyone who had the ability and will to act in this way, to oppose in this or other ways the machine of the Lager, was beyond the reach of "shame"—or at least the shame of which I am speaking, because perhaps he experiences something else.

Equally protected must have been Sivadjan, a silent and tranquil man whom I mentioned in passing in *Survival in Auschwitz*, in the chapter "The Canto of Ulysses," and about whom I discovered on that same occasion that he had brought explosives into the camp to foment a possible insurrection.

In my opinion, the feeling of shame or guilt that coincided with reacquired freedom was extremely composite: it contained diverse elements, and in diverse proportions for each individual. It must be remembered that each of us, both objectively and subjectively, lived the Lager in his own way.

Coming out of the darkness, one suffered because of the reacquired consciousness of having been diminished. Not by our will, cowardice, or fault, yet nevertheless we had lived for months and years at an animal level: our days had been encumbered from dawn to dusk by hunger, fatigue, cold, and fear, and any space for reflection, reasoning, experiencing emotions was wiped out. We endured filth, promiscuity, and destitution, suffering much less than we would have suffered from such things in normal life, because our moral yardstick had changed. Furthermore, all of us had stolen: in the kitchen, the factory, the camp, in short, "from the others," from the opposing side, but it was theft nevertheless. Some (few) had fallen so low as to steal bread from their own companions. We had not only forgotten our country and our culture, but also our family, our past, the future we had imagined for ourselves, because, like animals, we were confined to the present moment. Only at rare intervals did we come out of this condition of leveling, during the very few Sundays of rest, the fleeting minutes before falling asleep, or the fury of the air raids, but these were painful moments precisely because they gave us the opportunity to measure our diminishment from the outside.

I believe that it was precisely this turning to look back at the "perilous water" that gave rise to so many suicides after (sometimes immediately after) Liberation. It was in any case a critical moment which coincided with a flood of rethinking and depression. By contrast, all historians of the Lager—and also of the Soviet camps—agree in pointing out that cases of suicide *during* imprisonment were rare. Several explanations of this fact have been put forward; for my part I offer three, which are not mutually exclusive.

First of all, suicide is an act of man and not of the animal. It is a meditated act, a noninstinctive, unnatural choice, and in the Lager there were few opportunities to choose: people lived precisely like enslaved animals that sometimes let themselves die but do not kill themselves.

Secondly, "there were other things to think about," as the saying goes. The day was dense: one had to think about satisfying hunger, in some way elude fatigue and cold, avoid the blows. Precisely because of the constant imminence of death there was no time to concentrate on the idea of death. Svevo's remark in *Confessions of Zeno*, when he ruthlessly describes his father's agony, has the rawness of truth: "When one is dying, one is much too busy to think about death. All one's organism is devoted to breathing."

Thirdly, in the majority of cases, suicide is born from a feeling of guilt that no punishment has attenuated; now, the harshness of imprisonment was perceived as punishment, and the feeling of guilt (if there is punishment, there must have been guilt) was relegated to the background, only to re-emerge after the Liberation. In other words, there was no need to punish oneself by suicide because of a (true or presumed) guilt: one was already expiating it by one's daily suffering.

What guilt? When all was over, the awareness emerged that we had not done anything, or not enough, against the system into which we had been absorbed. About the failed resistance in the Lagers, or, more accurately, in some Lagers, too much has been said, too superficially, above all by people who had altogether different crimes to account for. Anyone who made the attempt knows that there existed situations, collective or personal, in which active resistance was possible, and others, much more frequent, in which it was not. It is known that, especially in 1941, millions of Soviet military prisoners fell into German hands. They were young, generally well nourished and robust; they had military and political training, and often they formed organic units with soldiers with the rank of corporal and up, noncommissioned officers, and officers. They hated the Germans who had invaded their country, and yet they rarely resisted. Malnutrition, despoilment, and other physical discomforts, which it is so easy and economically advantageous to provoke and at which the Nazis were masters, are rapidly destructive and paralyze before destroying, all the more so when they are preceded by years of segregation, humiliation, maltreatment, forced migration, laceration of family ties, rupture of contact with the rest of the world—that is to say, the situation of the bulk of the prisoners who had landed in Auschwitz after the introductory hell of the ghettos or the collection camps.

Therefore, on a rational plane, there should not have been much to be ashamed of, but shame persisted nevertheless, especially for the few bright examples of those who had the strength and possibility to resist. I spoke about this in the chapter "The Last" in *Survival in Auschwitz*, where I described the public hanging of a resistor before a terrified and apathetic crowd of prisoners. This is a thought that then just barely grazed us, but that returned "afterward": you too could have, you certainly should have. And this is a judgment that the survivor believes he sees in the eyes of those (especially the young) who listen to his stories and judge with facile hindsight, or who perhaps feel cruelly repelled. Consciously or not, he feels accused and judged, compelled to justify and defend himself.

More realistic is self-accusation, or the accusation of having failed in terms of human solidarity. Few survivors feel guilty about having deliberately damaged, robbed, or beaten a companion. Those who did so (the *Kapos*, but not only they) block out the memory. By contrast, however, almost everybody feels guilty of having omitted to offer help. The presence at your side of a weaker—or less cunning, or older, or too young—companion, hounding you with his demands for help or with his simple presence, in itself an entreaty, is a constant in the life of the Lager. The demand for solidarity, for a human word, advice, even just a listening ear, was permanent and universal but rarely satisfied. There was no time, space, privacy, patience, strength; most often, the person to whom the request was addressed found himself in his turn in a state of need, entitled to comfort.

I remember with a certain relief that I once tried to give courage (at a moment when I felt I had some) to an eighteen-year-old Italian who had just arrived, who was floundering in the bottomless despair of his first days in camp. I forget what I told him, certainly words of hope, perhaps a few lies, acceptable to a "new arrival," expressed with the authority of my twenty-five years and my three months of seniority; at any rate, I made him the gift of a momentary attention. But I also remember, with disquiet, that much more often I shrugged my shoulders impatiently at other requests, and this precisely when I had been in camp for almost a year and so had accumulated a good store of experience: but I had also deeply assimilated the principal rule of the place, which made it mandatory that you

take care of yourself first of all. I never found this rule
expressed with as much frankness as in *Prisoners of Fear*
by Ella Lingens-Reiner (where, however, the woman doctor, regardless of her own statement, proved to be generous and brave and saved many lives): "How was I able
to survive in Auschwitz? My principle is: I come first, second, and third. Then nothing, then again I; and then all the
others."

In August of 1944 it was very hot in Auschwitz. A tor-
rid, tropical wind lifted clouds of dust from the buildings
wrecked by the air raids, dried the sweat on our skin, and
thickened the blood in our veins. My squad had been sent
into a cellar to clear out the plaster rubble, and we all
suffered from thirst: a new suffering, which was added to,
indeed, multiplied by the old one of hunger. There was
no drinkable water in the camp or often on the work site;
in those days there was often no water in the wash trough
either, undrinkable but good enough to freshen up and
clean off the dust. As a rule, the evening soup and the
ersatz coffee distributed around ten o'clock were abun-
dantly sufficient to quench our thirst, but now they were
no longer enough and thirst tormented us. Thirst is more
imperative than hunger: hunger obeys the nerves, grants
remission, can be temporarily obliterated by an emotion,
a pain, a fear (we had realized this during our journey
by train from Italy); not so with thirst, which does not
give respite. Hunger exhausts, thirst enrages; in those days
it accompanied us day and night: by day, on the work site,
whose order (our enemy, but nevertheless order, a place
of logic and certainty) was transformed into a chaos of
shattered constructions; by night, in the hut without ven-
tilation, as we gasped the air breathed a hundred times
before.

The corner of the cellar that had been assigned to me

by the *Kapo* and where I was to remove the rubble was next to a large room filled with chemical equipment in the process of being installed but already damaged by the bombs. Along the vertical wall ran a two-inch pipe, which ended in a spigot just above the floor. A water pipe? I took a chance and tried to open it. I was alone, nobody saw me. It was blocked, but using a stone for a hammer I managed to shift it a few millimeters. A few drops came out, they had no odor, I caught them on my fingers: it really seemed water. I had no receptacle, and the drops came out slowly, without pressure: the pipe must be only half full, perhaps less. I stretched out on the floor with my mouth under the spigot, not trying to open it further: it was water made tepid by the sun, insipid, perhaps distilled or the result of condensation; at any rate, a delight.

How much water can a two-inch pipe one or two meters high contain? A liter, perhaps not even that. I could have drunk all of it immediately; that would have been the safest way. Or save a bit for the next day. Or share half of it with Alberto. Or reveal the secret to the whole squad. I chose the third path, that of selfishness extended to the person closest to you, which in distant times a friend of mine appropriately called us-ism. We drank all the water, in small, avaricious gulps, changing places under the spigot, just the two of us. On the sly. But on the march back to camp at my side I found Daniele, all gray with cement dust, his lips cracked and his eyes feverish, and I felt guilty. I exchanged a look with Alberto; we understood each other immediately and hoped nobody had seen us. But Daniele had caught a glimpse of us in that strange position, supine near the wall among the rubble, and had suspected something, and then had guessed. He curtly told me so many months later, in Byelorussia, after the Liberation: Why the two of you and not I? It was the "civilian" moral code surfacing again. The same according to which I the free man of today perceive as horrifying the death sentence of the sadistic *Kapo*, decided upon and executed without appeal, silently, with the stroke of an eraser. Is this belated shame justified or not? I was not able to decide then and I am not able to decide even now, but shame there was and is, concrete, heavy, perennial. Daniele is dead now, but in our meetings as survivors, fraternal, affectionate, the veil of that act of omission, that unshared glass of water, stood between us, transparent, not expressed, but perceptible and "costly."

Changing moral codes is always costly: all heretics, apostates, and dissidents know this. We cannot judge our behavior or that of others, driven at that time by the code of that time, on the basis of today's code; but the anger that pervades us when one of the "others" feels entitled to consider us "apostates," or, more precisely, reconverted, seems right to me.

Are you ashamed because you are alive in place of another? And in particular, of a man more generous, more sensitive, more useful, wiser, worthier of living than you? You cannot block out such feelings: you examine yourself, you review your memories, hoping to find them all, and that none of them are masked or disguised. No, you find no obvious transgressions, you did not usurp anyone's place, you did not beat anyone (but would you have had the strength to do so?), you did not accept positions (but none were offered to you . . .), you did not steal anyone's bread; nevertheless you cannot exclude it. It is no more than a supposition, indeed the shadow of a suspicion: that each man is his brother's Cain, that each one of us (but this time I say "us" in a much vaster, indeed, universal sense) has usurped his neighbor's place and lived in his stead. It is a supposition, but it gnaws at us; it has nestled deeply like a woodworm; although unseen from the outside, it gnaws and rasps.

After my return from imprisonment I was visited by a friend older than myself, mild and intransigent, the cultivator of a personal religion, which, however, always seemed to me severe and serious. He was glad to find me alive and basically unhurt, perhaps matured and fortified, certainly enriched. He told me that my having survived could not be the work of chance, of an accumulation of fortunate circumstances (as I did then and still do maintain) but rather of Providence. I bore the mark, I was an elect: I, the nonbeliever, and even less of a believer after the season of Auschwitz, was a person touched by Grace, a saved man. And why me? It is impossible to know, he answered. Perhaps because I had to write, and by writing bear witness: Wasn't I in fact then, in 1946, writing a book about my imprisonment?

Such an opinion seemed monstrous to me. It pained me as when one touches an exposed nerve, and kindled the doubt I spoke of before: I might be alive in the place of another, at the expense of another; I might have usurped, that is, in fact, killed. The "saved" of the Lager were not the best, those predestined to do good, the bearers of a message: what I had seen and lived through proved the exact contrary. Preferably the worst survived, the selfish, the violent, the insensitive, the collaborators of the "gray zone," the spies. It was not a certain rule (there were none, nor are there certain rules in human matters), but it was nevertheless a rule. I felt innocent, yes, but enrolled among the saved and therefore in permanent search of a justification in my own eyes and those of others. The worst survived, that is, the fittest; the best all died.

Chaim died, a watchmaker from Krakow, a pious Jew who despite the language difficulties made an effort to understand and be understood, and explained to me, the foreigner, the essential rules for survival during the first crucial days of captivity; Szabo died, the taciturn Hungarian peasant who was almost two meters tall and so was the hungriest of all, and yet, as long as he had the strength, did not hesitate to help his weaker companions to pull and push; and Robert, a professor at the Sorbonne who spread courage and trust all around him, spoke five languages, wore himself out recording everything in his prodigious memory, and had he lived would have answered the questions which I do not know how to answer; and Baruch died, a longshoreman from Livorno, immediately, on the first day, because he had answered the first punch he had received with punches and was massacred by three *Kapos* in coalition. These, and innumerable others, died not despite their valor but because of it.

My religious friend had told me that I survived so that I could bear witness. I have done so, as best I could, and I also could not have done so; and I am still doing so, whenever the opportunity presents itself; but the thought that this testifying of mine could by itself gain for me the privilege of surviving and living for many years without serious problems troubles me because I cannot see any proportion between the privilege and its outcome.

I must repeat: we, the survivors, are not the true witnesses. This is an uncomfortable notion of which I have become conscious little by little, reading the memoirs of others and reading mine at a distance of years. We survivors are not only an exiguous but also an anomalous minority: we are those who by their prevarications or abilities or good luck did not touch bottom. Those who did so, those who saw the Gorgon, have not returned to tell about it or have returned mute, but they are the "Muslims," the submerged, the complete witnesses, the ones whose deposition would have a general significance. They are the rule, we are the exception. Under another sky, and returned from a similar and diverse slavery, Solzhenitsyn also noted: "Almost all those who served a long sentence and whom you congratulate because they are survivors are unquestionably *pridurki* or were such during the greater part of their imprisonment. Because Lagers are meant for extermination, this should not be forgotten."

In the language of that other concentrationary universe, the *pridurki* are the prisoners who, in one way or another, won a position of privilege, those we called the Prominent.

We who were favored by fate tried, with more or less wisdom, to recount not only our fate but also that of the others, indeed of the drowned; but this was a discourse "on behalf of third parties," the story of things seen at close hand, not experienced personally. The destruction brought to an end, the job completed, was not told by anyone, just as no one ever returned to describe his own death. Even if they had paper and pen, the drowned would not have testified because their death had begun before that of their body. Weeks and months before being snuffed out, they had already lost the ability to observe, to remember, to compare and express themselves. We speak in their stead, by proxy.

I could not say whether we did or do so out of a kind of moral obligation toward those who were silenced or in order to free ourselves of their memory; certainly we do it because of a strong and durable impulse. I do not believe that psychoanalysts (who have pounced upon our tangles with professional avidity) are competent to explain this impulse. Their knowledge has been built up and tested "outside," in the world that, for the sake of simplicity, we call civilian: psychoanalysis traces its phenomenology and tries to explain it; studies its deviations and tries to heal them. Their interpretations, even those of someone like Bruno Bettelheim, who went through the trials of the Lager, seem to me appproximate and simplified, as if someone wished to apply the theorems of plane geometry to the solution of spheric triangles. The mental mechanisms of the *Häftlinge* were different from ours; curiously, and in parallel, different also were their physiology and pathology. In the Lager colds and influenza were unknown, but one died, at times suddenly, from illnesses that the doctors never had an opportunity to study. Gastric ulcers and mental illnesses were healed (or became asymptomatic), but everyone suffered from an unceasing discomfort that polluted sleep and was nameless. To define this as a "neurosis" is reductive and ridiculous. Perhaps it would be more correct to see in it an atavistic anguish whose echo one hears in the second verse of Genesis: the anguish inscribed in everyone of the "tohu-bohu" of a deserted and empty universe crushed under the spirit of God but from which the spirit of man is absent: not yet born or already extinguished.

And there is another, vaster shame, the shame of the world. It has been memorably pronounced by John Donne, and quoted innumerable times, pertinently or not, that "no man is an island," and that every bell tolls for everyone. And yet there are those who, faced by the crime of others or their own, turn their backs so as not to see it and not feel touched by it. This is what the majority of Germans did during the twelve Hitlerian years, deluding themselves that not seeing was a way of not knowing, and that not knowing relieved them of their share of complicity or connivance. But we were denied the screen of willed ignorance, T. S. Eliot's "partial shelter": we were not able not to see. The ocean of pain, past and present, surrounded us, and its level rose from year to year until it almost submerged us. It was useless to close one's eyes or turn one's back to it because it was all around, in every direction, all the way to the horizon. It was not possible for us nor did we want to become islands; the just among us, neither more nor less numerous than in any other human group, felt remorse, shame, and pain for the misdeeds that others and not they had committed, and in which they felt involved, because they sensed that what had happened around them and in their presence, and in them, was irrevocable. Never again could it be cleansed; it would prove that man, the human species—we, in short—had the potential to construct an infinite enormity of pain, and that pain is the only force created from nothing, without cost and without effort. It is enough not to see, not to listen, not to act.

We are often asked, as if our past conferred a prophetic ability upon us, whether Auschwitz will return: whether, that is, other slaughters will take place, unilateral, systematic, mechanized, willed, at a governmental level, perpetrated upon innocent and defenseless populations and legitimized by the doctrine of contempt. Prophets, to our good fortune, we are not, but something can be said. That a similar tragedy, almost ignored in the West, did take place, in Cambodia, in about 1975. That the German slaughter could be set off—and after that feed on itself—out of a desire for servitude and smallness of soul, thanks to the concurrence of a number of factors (the state of war, German technological and organizational perfectionism, Hitler's will and inverted charisma, the lack in Germany of solid democratic roots), not very numerous, each of them indispensable but insufficient if taken singly. These factors can occur again and are already recurring in various parts of the world. The convergence again of all of them within ten or twenty years (there is no sense in speaking of a more remote future) is not very likely but also not impossible. In my opinion, a mass slaughter is particularly unlikely in the Western world, Japan, and also the Soviet Union: the Lagers of World War II are still part of the memory of many, on both the popular and governmental levels, and a sort of immunizational defense is at work which amply coincides with the shame of which I have spoken.

As to what might happen in other parts of the world, or later on, it is prudent to suspend judgment. And the nuclear apocalypse, certainly bilateral, probably instantaneous and definitive, is a greater and different horror, strange, new, which stands outside the theme I have chosen.

4

COMMUNICATING

I NEVER liked the term *incommunicability*, so fashionable in the 1970s, first of all because it is a linguistic horror, and secondly for more personal reasons.

In today's normal world, which by convention and contrast we call from time to time "civilized" or "free," one almost never encounters a total linguistic barrier, that is, finds oneself facing a human being with whom one must absolutely establish communication or die, and then is unable to do so.

A famous but incomplete example of this is in Antonioni's film *Red Desert*, when one night the protagonist meets a Turkish sailor who knows not a word of any language but his own and tries in vain to make himself understood. Incomplete because on both sides, the sailor's as well, the will to communicate exists, or, at least, the will to reject contact is lacking.

According to a theory fashionable during those years, which to me seems frivolous and irritating, "incommunicability" supposedly was an inevitable ingredient, a life sentence inherent to the human condition, particularly the life style of industrial society: we are monads, incapable of reciprocal messages, or capable only of truncated messages, false at their departure, misunderstood on their arrival. Discourse is fictitious, pure noise, a painted veil that conceals existential silence; we are alone, even (or especially) if we live in pairs. It seems to me that this lament originates in and points to mental laziness; certainly it encourages it, in a dangerous vicious circle. Except for cases of pathological incapacity, one can and must communicate, and thereby contribute in a useful and easy way to the peace of others and oneself, because silence, the absence of signals, is itself a signal, but an ambiguous one, and ambiguity generates anxiety and suspicion. To say that it is impossible to communicate is false; one always can. To refuse to communicate is a failing; we are biologically and socially predisposed to communication, and in particular to its highly evolved and noble form, which is language. All members of the human species speak, no nonhuman species knows how to speak.

From the standpoint of communication—indeed, of failed communication—we survivors have known a peculiar experience. It is an irksome habit of ours to intervene when someone (our children!) speaks about cold, hunger, or fatigue. What do you know about it? You should have gone through what we did. In general, for reasons of good taste and good neighborliness, we try to resist the temptation of such *miles gloriosus* interventions; nevertheless I find it imperative to intervene precisely when I hear people talking about failed or impossible communication. "You should have experienced ours." There can be no comparison to the tourist in Finland or Japan who finds interlocutors who do not speak his language but are professionally (or even spon-

taneously) polite or well intentioned and make an effort
to understand and help him. Besides, who, in what corner
of the world, cannot string together a few words of English? In any event the questions of tourists are few, always
the same, hence uncertainties are rare, and almost understanding each other can even be as amusing as a game.

Certainly more dramatic is the case of the Italian immi-
grant in America a hundred years ago, or the Turk, Mo-
roccan, or Pakistani in Germany or Sweden today. Here
we no longer have a brief exploration stripped of the unexpected, conducted down tracks well tested by the travel
agencies; it is perhaps a definitive transplanting, an insertion
into work which today is rarely elementary and in which
the comprehension of the spoken or written word is essential, entailing indispensable human relationships with neighbors, clerks, colleagues, and superiors, at work, on the street,
at the café, with foreign people whose customs are different
and who are often hostile. But there is no lack of correc-
tives. Capitalist society itself is intelligent enough to understand that here its interest coincides with the output of the
"guest worker" and therefore with his well-being and his
adjustment. He is granted permission to bring along his
family, that is, a piece of his country; for better or worse
one finds lodgings for him; he may (often must) attend
language school. The deaf-mute who got off the train receives help, perhaps without love, not without efficiency,
and he soon reacquires speech.

We saw incommunicability in a more radical manner. I
refer in particular to Italian, Yugoslav, and Greek deportees, to a lesser extent to the French, among whom many
were of Polish or German extraction, and some, being Alsatian, understood German quite well, and to many Hungarians who came from the countryside. For us Italians, the

collision with the linguistic barrier took place dramatically already before deportation, already in Italy, at the moment in which the functionaries of the Italian police, with visible reluctance, turned us over to the SS, who, in February 1944, took over the management of the processing camp in Fossili near Modena. We immediately realized, from our very first contacts with the contemptuous men with the black patches, that knowing or not knowing German was a watershed. Those who understood them and answered in an articulate manner could establish the semblance of a human relationship. To those who did not understand them the black men reacted in a manner that astonished and frightened us: an order that had been pronounced in the calm voice of a man who knows he will be obeyed was repeated word for word in a loud, angry voice, then screamed at the top of his lungs as if he were addressing a deaf person or indeed a domestic animal, more responsive to the tone than the content of the message.

If anyone hesitated (everyone hesitated because they did not understand and were terrorized) the blows fell, and it was obvious that they were a variant of the same language: use of the word to communicate thought, this necessary and sufficient mechanism for man to be man, had fallen into disuse. This was a signal: for those people we were no longer men. With us, as with cows or mules, there was no substantial difference between a scream and a punch. For a horse to run or stop, turn, pull or stop pulling, it is not necessary to come to terms with it, or give it detailed explanations; a dictionary of a dozen variously assorted but univocal signs is sufficient, be they acoustical, tactile, or visual: pulling on the reins, jabbing the spurs, screams, gestures, cracking the whip, trumpeting with the lips, slams on the back are all equally good. Speaking to it, just like speaking to oneself, would be a foolish act, or a ridiculous mawkishness: what would the horse understand anyway? In his book *Mauthausen* (La Pietra, Milan, 1977), Marsalek tells us that in this Lager, even more polyglot than Auschwitz, the rubber truncheon was called *der Dolmetcher*, the interpreter: the one who made himself understood to everybody.

In fact, an uncultivated man (and Hitler's Germans, and the SS in particular, were frightfully uncultivated; they had not been "cultivated," or had been badly cultivated) does not know how to distinguish clearly between those who do not understand his language and those who do not understand *tout court*. It had been driven into the young Nazis' heads that in the world there existed only one civilization, the German; all others, present or past, were acceptable only insofar as they contained some German elements. Thus, whoever did not understand or speak German was a barbarian by definition; if he insisted on expressing himself in his own language—indeed, his nonlanguage—he must be beaten into silence and put back in his place, pulling, carrying, and pushing, because he was not a *Mensch*, not a human being. An eloquent episode comes to mind. On the work site, the rookie *Kapo* of a squad composed mainly of Italians, French, and Greeks, had not realized that one of the most feared SS supervisors had approached him from the back. He turned around abruptly, stood at attention, completely bewildered, and pronounced the prescribed *Meldung:* "83rd Kommando, forty-two men." Flustered as he was, he had actually said "*Zweiundvierzig Mann,*" "men." The SS corrected him in a reproachful, paternal tone: that's not what you say, you say "*Zweiundvierzig Häftlinge,*" forty-two prisoners. He was a young *Kapo* and therefore forgivable, but he must learn the trade, the social conventions, and hierarchical distances.

This "not being talked to" had rapid and devastating effects. To those who do not talk to you, or address you in screams that seem inarticulate to you, you do not dare speak. If you are fortunate enough to have next to you someone with whom you have a language in common, good for you, you'll be able to exchange your impressions, seek counsel, let off steam, confide in him; if you don't find anyone, your tongue dries up in a few days, and your thought with it.

Besides, on the immediate plane, you do not understand orders and prohibitions, do not decipher instructions, some futile and absurd, others fundamental. In short, you find yourself in a void, and you understand at your expense that communication generates information and that without information you cannot live. The greater part of the prisoners who did not understand German—that is, almost all the Italians—died during the first ten to fifteen days after their arrival: at first glance, from hunger, cold, fatigue, and disease; but after a more attentive examination, due to insufficient information. If they had been able to communicate with their more experienced companions, they would have been able to orient themselves better: to learn first of all how to procure clothing, shoes, illegal food, how to avoid the harsher labor and the often lethal encounters with the SS, how to handle the inevitable illnesses without making fatal mistakes. I don't mean to say that they would not have died, but they would have lived longer and had a greater chance of regaining lost ground.

For all of us survivors, who are not exactly polyglot, the first days in the Lager remain impressed in our memories like an out-of-focus and frenzied film, filled with a dreadful sound and fury signifying nothing: a hubbub of people without names or faces drowned in a continuous, deafening background noise from which, however, the human word did not surface. A black and white film, with sound but not a talkie.

I have noticed, in myself and others who came back, a curious effect of this void and need for communication. At a distance of forty years we still remember, in a purely acoustic form, words and sentences pronounced around us in languages we did not know and did not learn afterward: in my case, for example, in Polish or Hungarian. To this day I remember how one pronounced in Polish not my registration number but that of the prisoner who preceded me on the roster of a certain hut: a tangle of sounds that ended harmoniously, like the indecipherable counting jingles of children, in something like: "stergishi steri" (today I know that these two words mean "forty-four"). As a matter of fact, in that hut the soup dispenser and the greater part of the prisoners were Polish, and Polish was the official language; when you were called, you must be there ready, holding out your bowl in order not to miss your turn and, so as not to be caught by surprise, it was a good idea to jump when the companion with the immediately preceding registration number was called. In fact, that "stergishi steri" functioned like the bell that conditioned Pavlov's dogs: it stimulated an immediate secretion of saliva.

These foreign voices became engraved on our memories as on a blank tape; in the same manner, a famished stomach rapidly assimilates even indigestible food. Their meaning did not help us remember them because for us they had none; and yet, much later, we recited them to people who could understand them, and they did have a meaning, tenuous and banal: they were imprecations, curses, or small everyday, often repeated sentences, such as "What time is it?" or "I can't walk," or "Leave me alone." They were fragments torn from the indistinct, the fruit of a useless and unconscious effort to carve a meaning or sense out of the senseless. They also were the mental equivalent of our bodily need for nourishment, which drove us to search for potato peelings around the kitchens: little more than nothing, better than nothing. Also the undernourished brain suffers from a specific hunger of its own. Or perhaps this useless and paradoxical memory had another significance and purpose: it was the unconscious preparation for "later," for an improbable survival, in which every shred of experience would become a tessera in a vast mosaic.

In the first pages of *The Reawakening*, I described an extreme case of necessary and failed communication: that of the three-year-old child Hurbinek, perhaps born clandestinely in the Lager, whom nobody had taught to speak and who had an intense need to speak, expressed by his entire poor body. Even from this point of view, the Lager was a cruel laboratory in which one could witness situations and behaviors never seen before or after or anywhere else.

A few years earlier I had learned some German words, when I was still a student, for the sole purpose of understanding textbooks of chemistry and physics: certainly not to actively transmit my thought or understand the spoken language. Those were the years of the Fascist racial laws, and my meeting a German, or taking a trip to Germany, seemed quite improbable events. Flung into Auschwitz, despite my initial bewilderment (actually, perhaps indeed thanks to it) I soon understood that my extremely meager *Wortschatz* had become an essential factor of survival. *Wortschatz* means "lexical patrimony," but, literally, "treasure of words"; never was a term more appropriate. Knowing German meant life: I only had to look around me. My

Italian companions did not understand it, that is, almost all
with the exception of a few from Trieste were drowning
one by one in the stormy sea of not-understanding: they
did not know what the orders meant, they received slaps
and kicks without comprehending why. The camp's rudi-
mentary ethic stipulated that a blow must in some way be
justified, so as to facilitate the establishment of the trans-
gression-punishment-repentance parabola; therefore, often
the *Kapo* or his substitutes accompanied the blow with a
grunt: "You know why?" which was followed by a summary "communication of the crime." But for the newly
deaf and dumb this ceremonial was useless. They instinctively sought refuge in corners to protect their backs; aggression could come from any direction. They looked
around them with bewildered eyes, like trapped animals,
and that is what they had in fact become.

For many Italians the help of French and Spanish companions whose languages were less "foreign" than German
was vital. In Auschwitz there were no Spaniards, whereas
the French (more precisely, the deportees from France or
Belgium) were many, perhaps 10 percent of the total in
1944. Some were Alsatians, or German or Polish Jews who
during the preceding decade had sought a refuge in France
that turned out to be a trap: all of these knew German or
Yiddish, well or badly. The others, metropolitan French,
proletarians or bourgeois or intellectuals, had one or two
years earlier been subjected to a selection analogous to
ours: those who did not understand had disappeared from
the scene. Those who remained, almost all *métèques*, in the
past received rather grudgingly in France, had taken a sad
revanche. They were our natural interpreters: they translated for us the fundamental commands and warnings of
the day, "Get up," "Assembly," "Line up for bread,"

"Who's got broken shoes?" "By threes," "By fives," et cetera.

Certainly this was not enough. I implored one of them, an Alsatian, to give me a private and accelerated course, spread over brief lessons administered in a whisper, between the moment of curfew and the moment when we gave way to sleep, lessons to be recompensed with bread, since there was no other currency. He accepted, and I believe that never was bread better spent. He explained to me what the roars of the *Kapos* and SS meant, the foolish or ironic mottoes written in Gothic letters on the hut's roof trusses, the meaning of the colors of the triangles we wore on our chests above the registration number. So I realized that the German of the Lager—skeletal, howled, studded with obscenities and imprecations—was only vaguely related to the precise, austere language of my chemistry books, or to the melodious, refined German of Heine's poetry that Clara, a classmate of mine, used to recite to me.

I did not realize—I realized this only much later—that the Lager's German was a language apart: to say it precisely in German, it was *Orts- und zeitgebunden*, "tied to the place and time." It was a variant, particularly barbarized, of what a German Jewish philologist, Klemperer, had called *Lingua Tertii Imperii*, the language of the Third Reich, actually proposing for it the acronym LTI with an ironic analogy to the hundred other acronyms (NSDAP, SS, SA, SD, KZ, RKPA, WVHA, RSHA, BDM, etc.) dear to the Germany of that time.

About LTI, and its Italian equivalent, much has already been written, also by linguists. It is an obvious observation that where violence is inflicted on man it is also inflicted on language. In Italy we have not forgotten the foolish Fascist campaigns against the dialects, against "barbarisms," against the Valdostan, Valsusan, and Altoatesin place names, against the "*lei* form of address, servile and foreign." In Germany things were otherwise: already for centuries the German language had shown a spontaneous aversion to words of non-German origin, so that German scientists had rushed to rename bronchitis as "air-pipes inflammation," the duodenum as "twelve-finger intestine," and pyruvic acid as "burn-grapes acid." Therefore, from this point of view, Nazism, which wanted to purify everything, had very little left to purify. LTI differed from Goethe's German chiefly in certain semantic shifts and the abuse of certain terms. For example, the adjective *volkisch* ("national folk") had become omnipresent and laden with nationalistic arrogance, and the connotations of the adjective *fanatisch* had changed from negative to positive. But in the archipelago of German Lagers there had taken shape a sectorial language, a jargon, the "Lager jargon," subdivided into specific subjargons peculiar to each Lager and closely related to the old German of Prussian barracks and the new German of the SS. It is not surprising that it has been proven to run parallel to the jargon of Soviet labor camps, several terms of which are cited by Solzhenitsyn: every one of these has an exact counterpart in Lager jargon. The German translation of *The Gulag Archipelago* must not have presented many difficulties; or if it did, not those of terminology.

Common to all Lagers was the term *Muselmann*, "Muslim," given to the irreversibly exhausted, worn out prisoner close to death. Two explanations for it have been advanced, neither very convincing: fatalism; and the head bandages that could resemble a turban. It is mirrored exactly, even in its cynical irony, by the Russian term *dokodjaga*, literally "come to an end," "concluded." In the Ravensbrück Lager (the only one exclusively for women) the same concept

was expressed, so I'm told by Lydia Rolfi, by the two spec-
ular substantives *Schmutzstück* and *Schmuckstück*, respectively, "garbage" and "jewel," almost homophonous, one
the parody of the other. The Italian women did not understand their chilling significance, and unified the two terms
in one, pronouncing it "smistig." Also, "Prominent" is a
term common to all the subjargons. Concerning the "Prominent," the prisoners who had come up in the world, I've
spoken at length in *Survival in Auschwitz;* being an indispensable component of camp sociology they existed also
in the Soviet camps, where (as I mentioned in Chapter 3)
they were called *pridurki.*

In Auschwitz "to eat" was rendered *fressen,* a verb which
in good German is applied only to animals. For "go away"
the expression *hau' ab* was used, the imperative mode of
the verb *abhauen;* in proper German, this means "to cut,
chop off," but in Lager jargon it was equivalent to "go to
hell, get out of the way." I once happened to use this
expression (*Jetzt hauen wir ab*) in good faith shortly after
the end of the war to take leave of certain well-mannered
functionaries of the Bayer Company after a business meeting. It was as if I had said, "Now let's get the hell out of
here." They looked at me with astonishment: the term
belonged to a linguistic register different from that in which
our preceding conversation had been conducted and is certainly not taught in "foreign language" courses. I explained
to them that I had not learned German in school but rather
in a Lager called Auschwitz; this gave rise to a certain embarrassment, but since I was in the role of buyer they
continued to treat me with courtesy. I later on realized
also that my pronunciation is coarse, but I deliberately have
not tried to make it more genteel; for the same reason, I
have never had the tattoo removed from my left arm.

Lager jargon, as is only natural, was strongly influenced by other languages spoken in the Lager and its surroundings: Polish, Yiddish, Silesian dialect, later on Hungarian. From the background racket of my first days of imprisonment there immediately emerged, with insistence, four or five expressions that were not German; they must, I thought, indicate some basic object or activity, such as work, water, and bread. They became engraved in my memory, in the curious mechanical manner I described before. Only much later a Polish friend unwillingly explained to me that they simply meant "cholera," "blood of a dog," "thunder," "son of a whore," and "screwed," the first three having the function of exclamations.

Yiddish was de facto the camp's second language (replaced later on by Hungarian). Not only did I not understand it, I only vaguely knew about its existence, based on some quotation or joke heard from my father, who had worked for a few years in Hungary. The Polish, Russian, and Hungarian Jews were astonished that we Italians did not speak it: we were suspect Jews, not to be trusted, besides being, naturally, "badoghlios" for the SS and "mussolinis" for the French, Greeks, and political prisoners. Also, leaving aside the problems of communication, it was not comfortable being an Italian Jew. As is by now well known since the deserved success of the books of the Singer brothers and others, Yiddish is substantially an ancient German dialect, different from modern German both in lexicon and pronunciation. It caused me greater anguish than Polish, which I did not understand at all, because I should have understood it. I listened to it with strained attentiveness: often it was difficult for me to understand whether a sentence addressed to me or spoken near me was German or Yiddish or a hybrid: in fact, some well-intentioned Polish Jews made an effort to Germanize their Yiddish as much as they could so I could understand them.

Of the Yiddish breathed in with the air, I found a singular trace in *Survival in Auschwitz*. In the chapter entitled "Kraus," a dialogue is reported: Gounan, a French Jew of Polish extraction, addresses the Hungarian Kraus with the sentence, "Langsam, du blöder Einer, langsam, verstanden?" which translated word by word is "Slow, you stupid one, slow, understood?" It did sound a bit strange, but I really thought I had heard it like that (these were recent memories, I was writing in 1946), and I transcribed it just like that. My German translator was very doubtful: I must have heard or remembered incorrectly. After a long epistolary discussion, he suggested that the expression be altered, it did not appear acceptable to him. In fact, in the translation that was then published it goes like this: "Langsam, du blöder Heini . . ." where Heini is the diminutive of Heinrich, Henry. But recently in a fine book about the history and structure of Yiddish, *Mama loshen* by J. Geipel, I found that the form "Khamoyer du einer!" "Dunce you one!" is typical of the language. Mechanical memory had functioned correctly.

Not all suffered to the same extent because of failed or limited communication. Not to suffer from it, to accept the eclipse of the word, was an ominous symptom: it signaled the approach of definitive indifference. A few, solitary by nature, or already habituated to isolation in their "civilian" life, gave no sign of suffering from it, but the greater part of the prisoners who had overcome the critical phase of initiation tried to protect themselves, each in his own way: some begging for shreds of information; some spreading without discernment triumphant or disastrous information, true, false, or invented; some who sharpened eyes and ears to seize and try to interpret all signs offered by men, the earth, and the heavens. But to the limited internal communication was added the limited communication with the external world. In several Lagers isolation was total; mine, Monowitz-Auschwitz, could be considered privileged from this standpoint. Almost every week "new" prisoners arrived from all the countries of occupied Europe and brought with them recent news, often as eyewitnesses. In spite of prohibitions and the danger of being denounced to the Gestapo, on the huge work site we spoke with Polish and German workers, at times even with English prisoners of war; in the garbage cans we found newspapers that were a few days old and read them avidly. An enterprising work companion of mine, bilingual because he was Alsatian and a journalist by profession, even boasted of having taken out a subscription for the *Völkischer Beobachter*, the most authoritative daily German newspaper of the time: what could be easier? He had begged a trustworthy German worker to subscribe and had taken over the subscription by giving him a gold tooth. Every morning, during the long wait of roll call, he gathered us together and gave us an accurate summary of the day's news.

On June 7, 1944, we saw the English prisoners on their way to work, and there was something different about them: they marched well aligned, chests thrust forward, smiling, martial, with a step so eager that the German sentinel who escorted them, a no longer young territorial, had difficulty keeping up with them. They saluted us with the V sign of victory. The next day we found out that from a clandestine radio of theirs they had learned about the Allied landing in Normandy, and that was a great day for us, too: freedom seemed within reach. But in most camps things were much worse. The newcomers arrived from other Lagers or ghettos, which in turn were cut off from the world and so brought with them only the horrendous local news. Work did not, as with us, take place in contact with free workers from ten or twelve different countries, but on farms, small workshops, stone or sand quarries, even mines, and in the mine-Lagers conditions were the same that led to the death of the Romans' war slaves and the Indios subjugated by the Spanish: so lethal that no one returned to describe them. As I said before, the news "from the world" that reached us was sporadic and vague. We felt forgotten, like the condemned left to die in the medieval *oubliettes*.

The Jews, enemies by definition, impure and sowers of impurity, destroyers of the world, were forbidden that most precious communication, contact with their country of origin and their family: whoever has experienced exile, in any of its many forms, knows how much one suffers when this nerve is severed. It leads to a deadly impression of desertion and also to unjust resentment: Why don't they write to me? Why don't they help me, they who are free? We were able to understand very well, then, that on the great continent of freedom, freedom of communication is an important province. As with health, only the person who loses it realizes its true value. But one does not suffer from it only on an individual level: in countries and epochs in which communication is impeded, soon all other liberties wither; discussion dies by inanition, ignorance of the opinion of others becomes rampant, imposed opinions triumph. The well-known example of this is the crazy genetics preached in the USSR by Lysenko, which in the absence of discussion (his opponents were exiled to Siberia) compromised the harvests for twenty years. Intolerance is inclined to censor, and censorship promotes ignorance of the arguments of others and thus intolerance itself: a rigid, vicious circle that is hard to break.

The weekly hour when our "political" companions received mail from home was for us the saddest, when we felt the whole burden of being different, estranged, cut off from our country, indeed from the human race. It was the hour when we felt the tattoo burn like a wound, and the certainty that none of us would return overwhelmed us like an avalanche of mud. In any case, even if we had been allowed to write a letter—to whom would we have addressed it? The families of the Jews of Europe had been submerged or dispersed or destroyed.

I was given the rare good fortune (I told about it in *Moments of Reprieve*) of being able to exchange some letters with my family. For this I am indebted to two persons very different from each other: an old, almost illiterate bricklayer and a courageous young woman, Bianca Guidetta Serra, who is now a well-known attorney. I know that this was one of the factors that allowed me to survive, but, as I said before, each of us survivors is in more than one way an exception, a fact that we ourselves, to exorcize the past, tend to forget.

5

USELESS VIOLENCE

THE title of this chapter may seem provocative or even offensive: Is there such a thing as useful violence? Unfortunately, yes. Death, even when not provoked, even the most clement, is a violence, but it is sadly useful: a world of immortals (Swift's Strulbruggs) would be neither conceivable nor livable, would be more violent than the present life, violent though it is. Nor in general is murder useless: Raskolnikov, in killing the old moneylender, set a purpose for himself, albeit a culpable one; and so did Princip at Sarajevo and Aldo Moro's kidnappers in Via Fani. Leaving aside the cases of homicidal madness, anyone who kills knows why he does so: for money, to eliminate a true or presumed enemy, to avenge an insult. Wars are detestable, they are a very bad way to settle controversies between nations or factions, but they cannot be called useless: they aim at a goal, although it may be wicked or perverse. They are not gratuitous, their purpose is not to inflict suffering; suffering is there, it is collective, anguishing, unjust, but it is a by-product, something extra. Now, I believe that the twelve Hitlerian years shared their violence with many other historical space-times, but they were characterized by widespread useless violence, as an end in itself, with the sole purpose of inflicting pain, occasionally having a purpose, yet always redundant, always disporportionate to the purpose itself.

Thinking back with the wisdom of hindsight to those years that devastated Europe and, in the end, Germany itself, one feels torn between two opinions: Were we witnessing the rational development of an inhuman plan or a manifestation (unique in history and still unsatisfactorily explained) of collective madness? Logic intent on evil or the absence of logic? As so often happens in human affairs, the two alternatives coexisted. There is no doubt that the fundamental design of National Socialism had a rationale of its own: the eastward drive (an old German dream); stifling the workers' movement; hegemony over continental Europe; annihilation of Bolshevism and Judaism, which Hitler simplistically identified with one another; sharing world power with England and the United States; the apotheosis of the Germanic race with the "Spartan" elimination of the mentally ill and useless mouths. All these elements were mutually compatible and can be deduced from a few postulates already presented with undeniable clarity in *Mein Kampf:* Arrogance and radicalism, hubris and *Gründlichkeit* (thoroughness); insolent logic, not insanity.

Hateful but not insane were also the means foreseen to achieve these ends: to unleash military aggressions or ruthless wars, to support internal fifth columns, to transfer or remove entire populations, to subjugate, sterilize, or exterminate them. Neither Nietzsche nor Hitler nor Rosenberg were mad when they intoxicated themselves and their followers by preaching the myth of the Superman to whom everything is permitted in recognition of his dogmatic and congenital superiority, but worthy of meditation is the fact that all of them, teachers and pupils, became progressively removed from reality as little by little their morality came unglued from the morality common to all times and all civilizations, an integral part of our human heritage which in the end must be acknowledged.

Rationality ceases, and the disciples have amply surpassed (and betrayed!) the teacher, precisely in the practice of useless cruelty. Nietzsche's message is profoundly repugnant to me; I find it difficult to discover an affirmation in it which is not contrary to what I like to think. His oracular tone irritates me, yet it seems to me that a desire for the sufferings of others cannot be found in it. Indifference, yes, almost on every page, but never *Schadenfreude*, the joy in your neighbor's misfortune, and, even less, joy in deliberately inflicting suffering. The pain of the hoi polloi, of the *Ungestalten*, the shapeless, the not-born-noble, is a price that must be paid for the advent of the reign of the elect; it is a minor evil, but an evil nonetheless; it is not in itself desirable. Hitlerian doctrine and practice were much different.

Many of the useless Nazi violences by now belong to history: it is enough to think of the "disproportionate" massacres of the Ardeatine Caves, of Oradour, Lidice, Boves, Marzabotto and too many more, in which the limits of reprisal, already intrinsically inhuman, were enormously surpassed. But other minor, individual violences remain inscribed with indelible letters in the memory of each of us ex-deportees, details of the larger picture.

Almost always, at the beginning of the memory sequence, stands the train, which marked the departure toward the unknown, not only for chronological reasons but also for the gratuitous cruelty with which those (otherwise innocuous) convoys of ordinary freight cars were employed for an extraordinary purpose.

Among our many such accounts there is not a diary or story in which the train does not appear, the sealed boxcar converted from a commercial vehicle into an ambulatory prison or even an instrument of death. It is always packed, but the number of persons who, on each occasion, were jammed into it seems to be based on a rough calculation: from fifty to one hundred and twenty, depending on the length of the journey and the hierarchic level that the Nazi system assigned to the "human material" being transported. The convoys leaving from Italy contained "only" fifty to sixty persons per car (Jews, politicals, Partisans, unfortunates who had been rounded up on the streets, military personnel captured after the debacle of the eighth of September, 1943): it may be that distances were taken into account or perhaps even the impression that these trains would make on possible witnesses present along the route. At the opposite extreme stood the transports of Eastern Europe: Slavs, especially if Jewish, were lesser merchandise, indeed, almost totally devoid of value; they would in any case die, no matter whether during the journey or afterward. The convoys that transported Polish Jews from ghettos to Lagers, or from Lager to Lager, contained up to a hundred and twenty persons per car: their journey was brief. . . . Now, fifty persons in a freight car is most uncomfortable; they can all lie down simultaneously to rest, but body against body. If they are one hundred or more, even a trip of a few hours is an inferno: one must take turns standing or squatting, and often, among the travelers, there are old people, sick people, children, nursing women, lunatics, or individuals who go mad during or because of the journey.

Variables and constants can be distinguished in the procedure of Nazi railway transports. We cannot know whether this procedure was based on a regulation or whether the functionaries in charge had a free hand. Constant was the hypocritical advice (or order) to bring along as much as possible: especially gold, jewels, valuable currency, furs, in certain cases (certain transports of Jewish farmers from Hungary and Slovakia) even small livestock. "It's all stuff that will come in handy," the escort personnel said out of the side of their mouths and with an air of complicity. In fact, this was self-plunder, a simple and ingenious ruse to bring valuables into the Reich, without publicity, bureau-cratic complications, special transports, or fear of thefts en route—and sure enough, upon arrival, everything was seized. Constant was the total bareness of the cars; the German au-thorities, for a journey that might last as long as two weeks (as was the case with Jews deported from Salonika) liter-ally did not provide anything, neither foodstuffs, nor water, nor mats, nor straw to cover the wooden floor, nor recepta-cles for bodily needs, nor did they bother to alert the local authorities or the directors of the collection camps (when they existed) to provide these in some way or other. A no-tice would not have cost anything: rather, this systematic negligence became a useless cruelty, a deliberate creation of pain that was an end in itself.

In some cases the prisoners destined for deportation were able to learn something from experience: they had seen other convoys leave and learned at the expense of their predecessors that they themselves must take care of all these logistical necessities, as best they could, and compatibly with the limitations imposed by the Germans. Typical is the case of the trains that left from the collection camp of Wester-bork in the Netherlands. This was an enormous camp, with tens of thousands of Jewish prisoners, and Berlin expected the local commander to send off every week a train with approximately one thousand deportees: altogether, ninety-three trains left Westerbork headed for Auschwitz, Sobibor, and other minor camps. The survivors were approximately five hundred, and none of them traveled in the first convoys, whose occupants had departed blindly, with the unfounded hope that the more elementary needs for a three- or four-day journey would be administratively supplied; as a result, we don't know how many were those who died in transit, or how the terrifying journey unfolded, because no one returned to tell about it. But after a few weeks a staffer at the Westerbrook infirmary, a perspicacious observer, noticed that the boxcars of the convoys were always the same: they shuttled between the Lager of departure and the Lager of destination. So it happened that some among those who were deported after that were able to send messages hidden in the cars that returned empty, and from then on it was possible to provide at least some foodstuffs and water, and a barrel for excrement.

The convoy on which I was deported in February 1944 was the first to leave from the Fossoli collection camp. (Others had left earlier from Rome and Milan, but we had not heard about them.) The SS, who shortly before had ousted the Italian police from the camp management, gave no precise instructions for the journey; they only made it known that it would be long and they let trickle through the interested and ironic advice that I mentioned already ("Bring along gold and jewels, and above all woolen clothing and furs, because you're going to work in a cold country."). The head of the camp, he too a deportee, had the good sense to procure a reasonable supply of food, but not of water: water doesn't cost anything, isn't that so? The Germans don't give anything away, but they are good organizers. . . . Nor did he think to equip each boxcar with a receptacle to serve as a latrine, and this oversight proved to be most serious: it gave rise to a much worse affliction than thirst and cold. In my car there were quite a few old people, men and women, among others, all the inmates of the Jewish Rest Home of Venice. For everybody, but especially for them, evacuating in public was painful or even impossible: a trauma for which civilization does not prepare us, a deep wound inflicted on human dignity, an aggression which is obscene and ominous, but also the sign of deliberate and gratuitous viciousness. It was our paradoxical luck (although I hesitate to write this word in this context) that in our car there were also two young mothers with their infants of a few months and one of them had brought along a chamber pot: one only, and it had to serve about fifty people. Two days into the journey we found some nails stuck into the wooden sides, pushed two of them into a corner, and with a piece of string and a blanket improvised a screen, which was substantially symbolic: we are not yet animals, we will not be animals as long as we try to resist.

What happened in the other cars, which did not have this minimal equipment, is difficult to imagine. The convoy was stopped two or three times in the open countryside, the doors of the freight cars were opened, and the prisoners were allowed to get off—but not to walk away from the tracks or to go off on their own. The doors were opened another time, but during a stop in an Austrian railroad station. The SS escort did not hide their amusement at the sight of men and women squatting wherever they could, on the platforms and in the middle of the tracks, and the German passengers openly expressed their disgust: people like this deserve their fate, just look how they behave. These are not *Menschen*, human beings, but animals; it's clear as the light of day.

This was actually a prologue. In the life that was to follow, the daily rhythm of the Lager, the offense to modesty represented, at least at the beginning, an important part of the global suffering. It was neither easy nor painless to get used to the enormous collective latrine, at brief and obligatory times, in the presence, right in front of you, of the candidate to the succession; on his feet, impatient, at times pleading, at others bullying, every ten seconds insisting: "Hast du gemacht?" "Aren't you finished yet?" Nevertheless, within a few weeks, the discomfort became attenuated, and then vanished; in its place came (not for everyone) habituation, which is a charitable way of saying that the transformation from human beings into animals was well on its way. I do not believe that this transformation was ever planned or formulated in so many words at any level of the Nazi hierarchy, in any document, at any "labor meeting." It was a logical consequence of the system: an inhuman regime spreads and extends its inhumanity in all directions, also and especially downward; unless it meets with resistance and exceptionally strong characters, it corrupts its victims and its opponents as well. The useless cruelty of violated modesty conditioned the existence of all Lagers. The women of Birkenau tell how once having acquired a precious receptacle (a large bowl of enameled metal), they had to employ it for three distinct uses: to draw their soup; to evacuate into at night, when access to the latrines was forbidden; and to wash themselves when there was water at the troughs. In all camps, the alimentation included a liter of soup a day; in our Lager by concession of the chemical plant for which we worked we got two liters. So there was a lot of water to be eliminated, and this forced us to ask permission to go to the latrines frequently or manage otherwise in the corners of the work site. Some of the prisoners were unable to control themselves: due to bladder weakness, attacks of fear, neurosis, they were overcome by an urgent need to urinate and often wet themselves, and for this they were punished and derided. An Italian of my age, sleeping in the third tier of the bunk beds, had an accident one night and wet the occupants of the tier below, who immediately reported the event to the *Kapo* of the hut. He swooped down on the Italian, who, against all evidence, denied the charge. At that the *Kapo* ordered him to urinate there and then, to prove his innocence; naturally he did not succeed and was given a severe beating, but despite his reasonable request he was not transferred to a lower berth. This was an administrative act, which would have entailed too many complications for the hut's scribe.

Similar to the excremental coercion was the coercion of nudity. One entered the Lager naked: indeed, more than naked, deprived not only of clothing and shoes (which were confiscated) but of one's head of hair and all other hair. The same is or was done on entry into the military barracks, no doubt, but here the shaving was total and weekly, and public and collective nudity was a recurrent condition, typical and laden with significance. This too was a violence with some roots in necessity (clearly one must undress for a shower or a medical examination), but offensive because of its useless redundancy. The day in the Lager was studded with innumerable harsh strippings—checking for lice, searching one's clothes, examining for scabies and then the morning wash-up—as well as for the periodic selections, during which a "commission" decided who was still fit for work and who, on the contrary, was marked for elimination. Now a naked and barefoot man feels that all his nerves and tendons are severed: he is helpless prey. Clothes, even the foul clothes distributed, even the crude clogs with their wooden soles, are a tenuous but indispensable defense. Anyone who does not have them no longer perceives himself as a human being but rather as a worm: naked, slow, ignoble, prone on the ground. He knows that he can be crushed at any moment.

The same debilitating sensation of impotence and destitution was produced during the first days of imprisonment by the lack of a spoon: this is a detail that may appear marginal to those who since childhood are used to the abundance of cutlery at the disposal of even the poorest of kitchens, but it was not marginal. Without a spoon, the daily soup could not be consumed in any other way than by lapping it up, as dogs do; only after many days of apprenticeship (and here too how important it was to be immediately able to understand and make oneself understood!) one discovered that there were spoons in the camp but that one had to buy them on the black market with soup or bread: usually a spoon cost half a bread ration or a liter of soup, but inexperienced newcomers were always asked for much more. And yet, when the camp at Auschwitz was liberated, in the warehouse we found thousands of brand new transparent plastic spoons, besides tens of thousands of spoons made of aluminum, steel, or even silver that came from the luggage of deportees as they arrived. So it was not a matter of thrift but a precise intent to humiliate. The episode narrated in Judges 7:5 comes back to mind, in which the warrior Gideon chooses the best among his warriors by observing how they behave while drinking at the river: he rejects all those who lap up the water "as does the dog" or kneel, and accepts only those who drink standing up, lifting their hands to their mouths.

I would hesitate to define as totally useless other harassments and violences that have been repeatedly and concordantly described by all the Lager memorialists. It is well known that a roll call took place in all camps once or twice a day. It certainly was not a nominal roll call, which with thousands or tens of thousands of prisoners would have been impossible: all the more so because they were never referred to by name but only by the five or six digits on the registration number. It was *Zählappell*, a complicated and laborious counting-call because it had to take into consideration prisoners transferred to other camps or to the infirmary the evening before and those who had died during the night, and because the present number must square exactly with the figures of the preceding day, and the counting by fives took place as the squads headed for work filed by. Eugen Kogan reports that in Buchenwald also the dead and dying had to show up for the evening roll call; stretched out on the ground rather than on their feet, they too had to be aligned by fives, to facilitate the count.

This roll call took place (in the open, naturally) in all weather and lasted at least an hour, or even two or three if the count did not balance out—and even twenty-four hours or longer if an escape was suspected. When it rained or snowed, or the cold was intense, it became a torture, even worse than the labor to whose fatigue it was added in the evening: it was perceived as an empty and ritual ceremony, but probably it was not. It was not useless, as in any case, when seen from this angle, neither hunger nor exhausting labor were useless, and not even (may I be forgiven the cynicism: I am trying to reason with a logic that isn't mine) the death by gas of adults and children. All these sufferings were the development of a theme, that of the presumed right of a superior people to subjugate or eliminate an inferior people; such also was that roll call, which in our dreams of "afterward" had become the very emblem of the Lager, summing up in itself the fatigue, cold, hunger, and frustration. The suffering it caused, and which in the winter led every day to some breakdowns or some deaths, fit into the system, the tradition of the "drill" (English in original), the ferocious military practice which was a Prussian inheritance and which Buchner had immortalized in his play *Wozzeck*.

Besides, it seems evident to me that in many of its painful and absurd aspects the concentrationary world was only a version, an adaptation of German military procedures. The army of prisoners in the Lagers had to be an inglorious copy of the army proper—or, more accurately, its caricature. An army has a uniform: the soldier's uniform clean, honored, and covered with insignia, while that of the *Häftling* is filthy, dull, and gray—but both must have five buttons, or else there was trouble. An army marches by in military step, in close order, to the sound of a band; so too there must be a band in the Lager, and the march-past must be a march-past by the book, with "eyes left" before the reviewing stand and to the sound of music. This ceremony is so necessary, so obvious, as even to prevail over the anti-Jewish legislation of the Third Reich: with paranoid sophistry, this legislation prohibited Jewish orchestras and musicians from playing the scores of Aryan composers, whom they thereby would contaminate. But in the Lagers filled with Jews there were no Aryan musicians—nor, for that matter, are there many military marches written by Jewish composers—therefore, waiving the rules of purity, Auschwitz was the only German place where Jewish musicians could, indeed were compelled to play Aryan music: necessity knows no rules.

A barracks heritage also was the ritual of "making the beds." Of course, this locution is largely euphemistic; where there were bunk beds, each berth comprised a thin mattress filled with wood shavings, two blankets, and a straw pillow, and as a rule two people slept on it. The beds had to be made immediately after reveille, simultaneously throughout the hut, and it was therefore necessary for the occupants of the lower bunks to manage as best they could to fix mattress and blanket between the legs of the tenants of the upper levels, who were in precarious balance on the wooden rims and were also intent on the same job: all beds had to be put in order within a minute or two, because the bread distribution began immediately after. Those were frantic moments: the atmosphere filled with dust to the point of becoming opaque, with nervous tension and curses exchanged in all languages, because "making beds" (*Bettenbauen*, the technical term) was a sacral operation to be performed in accordance with iron rules. The mattress, fetid with mold and strewn with suspect stains, had to be fluffed up: for that purpose there existed two slits in the lining, through which one could insert the hands. One of the two blankets was supposed to be turned under the mattress and the other spread out over the pillow in such a way as to form a neat step, with sharp edges. When the operation was finished, the ensemble must look like a rectangular parallelepiped with well-smoothed edges, on which was placed the smaller parallelepiped of the pillow.

For the SS in the camp, and consequently for all barracks heads, *Bettenbauen* had a prime and indecipherable importance: perhaps it was a symbol of order and discipline. Anyone who did not make his bed properly, or forgot to make it, was punished publicly and savagely. Furthermore, in every barracks there existed a pair of functionaries, the *Bettnachzieher* ("bed after-pullers," a term that I believe does not exist in normal German and that Goethe certainly would not have understood), whose task it was to check every single bed and then take care of its transversal alignment. For this purpose, they were equipped with a string the length of the hut: they stretched it over the made-up beds, and rectified down to the centimeter any possible deviations. Rather than a cause of torment this maniacal order seemed absurd and grotesque: in fact, the mattress leveled out with so much care had no consistency whatever, and in the evening, under the body's weight, it immediately flattened down to the slats that supported it. In point of fact, one slept on wood.

Within much more extended limits, one gains the impression that throughout all of Hitlerian Germany the barracks code and etiquette replaced those which were traditional and "bourgeois": the insipid violence of the "drill" had already in 1934 begun to invade the field of education and had been turned against the German people themselves. Those newspapers of the period which had preserved a certain freedom in reporting and criticism describe exhausting marches imposed on adolescent boys and girls within the framework of premilitary exercises: up to fifty kilometers a day, with knapsacks on their backs and no pity for stragglers. Parents and doctors who dared to protest were threatened with political sanctions.

Altogether different is what must be said about the tattoo, an autochthonous Auschwitzian invention. From the beginning in 1942 in Auschwitz and the Lagers under its jurisdiction (in 1944 they were about forty) prisoner registration numbers were no longer only sewed to the clothes but tattooed on the left forearm. Only non-Jewish German prisoners were exempt from this rule. The operation was performed with methodical rapidity by specialized "scribes" at the moment of the new arrival's registration, when coming from freedom, other camps, or the ghettos. In deference to the typically German talent for classification, a true and proper code soon began to take shape: men were tattooed on the outside of the arm and women on the inside; the numbers of the *Zigeuner*, the gypsies, had to be preceded by a Z. The number of a Jew, starting in May 1944 (that is, with the mass arrival of Hungarian Jews) had to be preceded by an A, which shortly after was replaced by a B. Until September 1944 there were no children in Auschwitz; they were all killed by gas on arrival. After this date, there began to arrive entire families of Poles arrested at random during the Warsaw insurrection: all of them were tattooed, including newborn babies.

The operation was not very painful and lasted no more than a minute, but it was traumatic. Its symbolic meaning was clear to everyone: this is an indelible mark, you will never leave here; this is the mark with which slaves are branded and cattle sent to the slaughter, and that is what you have become. You no longer have a name; this is your new name. The violence of the tattoo was gratuitous, an end in itself, pure offense: were the three canvas numbers sewed to pants, jackets, and winter coat not enough? No, they were not enough: something more was needed, a nonverbal message, so that the innocent would feel his sentence written on his flesh. It was also a return to barbarism, all the more perturbing for Orthodox Jews: in fact, precisely in order to distinguish Jews from the barbarians, the tattoo is forbidden by Mosaic law (Leviticus 19:28).

At a distance of forty years, my tattoo has become a part of my body. I don't glory in it, but I am not ashamed of it either; I do not display and do not hide it. I show it unwillingly to those who ask out of pure curiosity; readily and with anger to those who say they are incredulous. Often young people ask me why I don't have it erased, and this surprises me: Why should I? There are not many of us in the world to bear this witness.

It is necessary to do (useful?) violence to oneself, to induce oneself to speak of the fate of the most helpless. I try once again to follow a logic that isn't mine. For an orthodox Nazi it must have been obvious, definitive, clear that all Jews should be killed: that was a dogma, a postulate. Also the children, of course: also and especially pregnant women, so that no future enemies should be born. But why, during the furious roundups in all the cities and villages of their boundless empire, why violate the houses of the dying? Why go to the trouble of dragging them onto their trains, take them to die far away, after a senseless journey, to die in Poland on the threshold of the gas chambers? In my convoy there were two dying ninety-year-old women, taken out of the Fossoli infirmary: one of them died en route, nursed in vain by her daughters. Would it not have been simpler, more "economical," to let them die, or perhaps kill them in their beds, instead of adding their agony to the collective agony of the transport? One is truly led to think that, in the Third Reich, the best choice, the choice imposed from above, was the one that entailed the greatest affliction, the greatest waste, the greatest physical and moral suffering. The "enemy" must not only die, he must die in torment.

Much has been written about work in the Lagers; I myself have described it in the past. Work was not paid; that is, it was slave work, one of the three purposes of the concentrationary system, the other two being the elimination of political adversaries and the extermination of the so-called inferior races. Let it be said in passing: the Soviet concentrationary regime differed from the Nazi regime

essentially by the absence of the third term and the preva-
lence of the first. In the early Lagers, which were almost
coeval with Hitler's coming to power, work was purely
persecutory, practically useless for productive ends: to
send the undernourished to dig up turf or cut stone served
only a terroristic purpose. At any rate, for Nazi and Fascist
rhetoric, in this the heir of bourgeois rhetoric, "work en-
nobles," and therefore the ignoble adversaries of the regime
are not worthy of working in the commonly accepted
meaning of the word. Their work must be afflictive: it must
leave no room for professionalism, must be the work *of*
beasts of burden—pull, push, carry weights, bend over the
soil. This too is useless violence: useful only to break down
current resistance and punish past resistance. The women of
Ravensbrück tell about interminable days during the quar-
antine period (before their incorporation in the factory
work squads) spent shoveling the sand of the dunes: in a
circle, under the July sun, each deportee had to move the
sand of her pile onto that of her neighbor on the right in
a pointless and endless merry-go-round, because the sand
ended up back where it came from.

But it is doubtful that this torment of body and spirit,
mythical and Dantesque, was excogitated to prevent the
formation of self-defense and active resistance nuclei: the
Lager SS were obtuse brutes, not subtle demons. They had
been raised to violence; violence ran in their veins. It was
normal, obvious. It could be seen in their faces, their gestures, their language. To humiliate, to make the "enemy"
suffer, was their everyday task; they did not reason about
it, they had no ulterior ends: their end was simply that. I
do not mean to say that they were made of a perverse human substance, different from ours (there were also sadists
and psychopaths among them, but they were few). Simply

enough, for a few years they had been subjected to a school in which current morality was turned upside down. In a totalitarian regime, education, propaganda, and information meet with no obstacles: they have an unlimited power about which anyone who was born and has lived in a pluralistic regime will find it difficult to form an idea.

Unlike the purely persecutory labor I have just described, work could instead at times become a defense, as it was for the few who in the Lager were made to exercise their own trade: tailors, cobblers, carpenters, blacksmiths, bricklayers. Such people, resuming their customary activity, recovered at the same time, to some extent, their human dignity. But it was this also for many others: an exercise of the mind, an escape from the thought of death, a way of living from day to day. In any case it is common experience that daily cares, even though painful or irksome, help take one's mind off more serious but more distant threats.

I frequently noticed in some of my companions (sometimes even in myself)a curious phenomenon: the ambition of a "job well done" is so deeply rooted as to compel one "to do well" even enemy jobs, harmful to your people and your side, so that a conscious effort is necessary to do them "badly." The sabotage of Nazi work, besides being dangerous, also meant overcoming atavistic inner resistances. The Fossano bricklayer who saved my life, and whom I described in *Survival in Auschwitz* and *Moments of Reprieve*, detested Germany, the Germans, their food, their language, their war; but when they set him to build protective walls against the aerial bombs he built them straight, solid, with well-staggered bricks and as much mortar as was required, not in deference to orders but out of professional dignity. In *A Day in the Life of Ivan Denisovich* Solzhenitsyn describes an almost identical situation: Ivan, the protagonist, sentenced though guiltless to ten years of forced labor, finds satisfaction in building a wall according to the highest standards of his trade, and then in realizing that it has turned out perfectly straight: Ivan "was made in that cretinous manner, nor had the eight years spent in prison camps caused him to lose that habit: he valued everything and every job of work and would not let them be spoiled unnecessarily." Those who saw the famous film *The Bridge on the River Kwai* will remember the absurd zeal with which the English officer, prisoner of the Japanese, strives to build an audacious wooden bridge for them and is shocked when he realizes that the English sappers have mined it. So you see, love for a job well done is a deeply ambiguous virtue. It animated Michelangelo through his last days, but then Stangl, that most diligent Treblinka henchman, answered an interviewer with irritation: "Everything I did of my own free will I had to do as best I could. That's how I am." Rudolph Höss, the Auschwitz commander, boasts of the same virtue when he describes the creative travail that led to his invention of the gas chambers.

Finally, as an extreme example of at once stupid and symbolic violence, I would like to mention the iniquitous use that was made (not sporadically but with method) of the human body as an object, an anonymous thing belonging to no one, to be disposed of in an arbitrary manner. About the medical experiments performed in Dachau, Auschwitz, Ravensbrück, and elsewhere much has already been written, and some of those responsible, who were not all physicians but often improvised as such, were even punished (not Josef Mengele, the most important and worst of all). The gamut of these experiments ranged from tests of new medications on unaware prisoners all the way to senseless and scientifically useless tortures, like those performed in Dachau, on Himmler's orders and on behalf of the Luft-waffe. Here, the chosen individuals, sometimes specially fed to be restored to their physiological normality, were subjected to long immersions in freezing water or intro-duced into decompression chambers in which air rarefac-tion at twenty thousand meters (an altitude that airplanes of the period were far from reaching!) was simulated in order to establish at what altitude human blood begins to boil: a datum that can be obtained in any laboratory at minimum expense and without victims, or even can be de-duced from common tables. It seems significant to me to recall these abominations at a time when, for good reason, there are discussions as to within what limits it is permissi-ble to perform painful scientific experiments on laboratory animals. This cruelty, typical and devoid of apparent pur-pose but highly symbolic, was extended, precisely because symbolic, to human remains after death: those remains which every civilization, beginning with remotest prehis-tory, has respected, honored, and sometimes feared. The treatment to which they were subjected in the Lagers was intended to declare that these were not human remains but indifferent brute matter, in the best of cases good for some industrial use. After decades, horror and revulsion are still aroused by the display case in the Auschwitz Museum where the hair cut from the women sent to the gas cham-bers or the Lagers is exhibited pell mell and by the ton: time has discolored and macerated it, but it continues to whisper its mute accusation to the visitor. The Germans did not have the time to send it on to its destination: this unusual merchandise was purchased by a number of Ger-man textile industries, which used it for the manufacture of mattress ticking and other industrial textiles. It is un-likely that those who utilized it did not know what sort of material this was. It is just as unlikely that the sellers, that is, the SS authorities of the Lager, actually made a profit from it: the outrage motive prevailed over the profit motive.

The human ashes coming from the crematoria, tons daily, were easily recognized as such, because they often contained teeth or vertebrae. Nevertheless, they were employed for several purposes: as fill for swamp lands, as thermal insulation between the walls of wooden buildings, and as phosphate fertilizer; and especially notable, they were used instead of gravel to cover the paths of the SS village located near the camp, whether out of pure callousness or because, due to their origins, they were regarded as material to be trampled on, I couldn't say.

I am under no illusion of having gone to the bottom of this question or of having demonstrated that useless cruelty is the exclusive appurtenance of the Third Reich and the necessary consequence of its ideological premises. What we know about Pol Pot's Cambodia, for example, suggests other explanations, but Cambodia is far from Europe and we know little about it, so how could we discuss it? Certainly, this was one of the fundamental features of Hitlerism not only inside the Lagers; and it seems to me that the best comment on it is summed up in these two remarks taken from a long interview by Gitta Sereny with the already mentioned Stangl, ex-commandant of Treblinka (*In quelle tenebre*, Adelphi, Milan, 1975, p. 135).

"Considering that you were going to kill them all . . . what was the point of the humiliations, the cruelties?" the writer asks Stangl, imprisoned for life in the Düsseldorf jail, and he replies: "To condition those who were to be the material executors of the operations. To make it possible for them to do what they were doing." In other words: before dying the victim must be degraded, so that the murderer will be less burdened by guilt. This is an explanation not devoid of logic but it shouts to heaven: it is the sole usefulness of useless violence.

6

THE INTELLECTUAL
IN AUSCHWITZ

To polemicize with a dead man is embarrassing and not very loyal, all the more so when the absent one is a potential friend and a most valuable interlocutor: but it can be an obligatory step. I speak about Hans Mayer, alias Jean Améry, the philosopher who committed suicide and a theoretician of suicide whom I already quoted in the Preface: between these two names extends his life without peace and without a search for peace. He was born in Vienna in 1912, in a family which was mainly Jewish but assimilated and integrated into the Austro-Hungarian Empire. Even though nobody had converted to Christianity with the due formalities, Christmas was celebrated in his house around a tree adorned with shiny ornaments; on the occasion of small domestic accidents, his mother invoked Jesus, Joseph and Mary, and the souvenir photograph of his father, who died at the front in World War I, showed not a wise, bearded Jew but an officer in the uniform of the Tyrolean Kaiserjäger. Until he was nineteen years old, Hans had never heard about the existence of a Yiddish language.

He obtained his degree in literature and philosophy in Vienna, not without some collisions with the nascent National Socialist party: to him being Jewish is not important, but for the Nazis his opinions and tendencies have no weight whatsoever; blood is the only thing that matters, and his is impure enough to make him an enemy of Germanism. A Nazi fist breaks one of his teeth, and the young intellectual is proud of the gap in his mouth, as if it were a scar received in a student duel. With the Nuremberg laws of 1935 and the subsequent annexation of Austria to Germany in 1938, his fate is at a crossroads and the young Hans, a skeptic and pessimist by nature, does not delude himself. He is sufficiently lucid (*Luzidität* will always be one of his favorite words) to understand early on that in German hands every Jew is "a dead man on vacation, a man to be murdered."

He does not consider himself Jewish: he does not know Hebrew or Hebrew culture, does not heed the Zionist doctrine; religiously he is an agnostic. Nor does he feel able to construct for himself an identity he does not have: that would be a falsification, a masquerade. Whoever was not born within the Jewish tradition is not a Jew and cannot easily become one: by definition, a tradition is inherited; it is the product of centuries, it cannot be fabricated *a posteriori*. And yet, in order to live, an identity—that is, dignity—is necessary. For him the two concepts coincide. Whoever loses one also loses the other, dies spiritually: without defenses he is therefore exposed also to physical death. Now, to him, as to many other German Jews who like him believed in German culture, the German identity was denied: by Nazi propaganda, on the obscene pages of Streicher's *Stürmer*, the Jew is described as a hairy parasite, fat, with crooked legs, a beaked nose, flapping ears, good only at harming others. German he is not, by axiom; indeed, his presence is sufficient to contaminate public baths and even park benches.

From this degradation, this *Entwürdigung*, it is impossible to protect oneself. The entire world watches it impassively; the German Jews themselves, almost all of them, succumb to the state's abuses and feel objectively degraded. His way of escaping this is paradoxical and contradictory: to accept one's destiny, in this case Judaism, and at the same time rebel against the imposed choice. For the young Hans, a prodigal Jew, being Jewish is simultaneously impossible and obligatory; his ambivalence, which will follow him until death and indeed provoke it, begins here. He denies possessing physical courage, but he does not lack moral courage: in 1938 he leaves his "annexed" country and emigrates to Belgium. From now on he will be Jean Améry, an almost-anagram of his original name. Out of dignity, and for no other reason, he will accept Judaism, but as a Jew "[he will travel] through the world as a man afflicted by one of those diseases which do not cause great suffering but are certain to have a lethal end." He, the cultivated German humanist and critic, tries to become a French writer (he will never succeed) and in Belgium joins a Resistance movement whose actual political hopes are negligible. His morality, for which he pays dearly in material and spiritual terms, by now has changed: at least symbolically it consists of "returning the blow."

In 1940 the Hitlerian tide submerges Belgium, too, and Jean, who despite his choice has remained a solitary and introverted intellectual, in 1943 falls into the hands of the Gestapo. He is asked to reveal the names of his comrades and his superiors, otherwise he will be tortured. He is not a hero; in his pages he honestly admits that if he had known them he would have talked, but he does not know them. His hands are tied behind his back and he is hung from a pulley by his wrists. After a few seconds his arms come out of their sockets and remain twisted upward, vertical behind his back. His torturers persevere, they savage the hanging body, which by now is unconscious, but Jean knows nothing, cannot even take refuge in betrayal. He is healed but is identified as a Jew and sent to Auschwitz-Monowitz, the same Lager in which I too would be imprisoned a few months later.

Even though we never saw each other again, after Liberation we exchanged several letters, having recognized, or more accurately, come to know, each other through our respective books. Our memories of "down there" coincide reasonably well on the plane of material details, but they diverge on one strange fact: I, who have always maintained that I preserve of Auschwitz a total, indelible memory, have forgotten his appearance; he declares that he remembers me, even though he confused me with Carlo Levi, who at that time was already well known in France as a political exile and painter. Indeed, he says that for a few weeks we lived in the same hut and that he did not forget me because the Italians were so few as to constitute a rarity, and furthermore, because in the Lager, during the last two months, I basically exercised my profession, that of chemist, and this was even a greater rarity.

This essay of mine would like to be at once a summary, a paraphrase, a discussion and critique of *his* bitter, gelid essay, which has two titles (*The Intellectual in Auschwitz* and *At the Limits of the Spirit*). It comes from a book that for many years I would have liked to translate. It too has two titles: *Beyond Guilt and Expiation* and *An Attempt to Overcome by One Overwhelmed.*

As one sees from the first title, the theme of Améry's essay is circumscribed with precision. Améry was in various Nazi prisons, and besides, after Auschwitz, he was briefly in Buchenwald and Bergen-Belsen, but his observations, for good reason, are confined to Auschwitz: the limits of the spirit, the nonimaginable, were there. Was being an intellectual in Auschwitz an advantage or a disadvantage?

Of course it is necessary to define what is meant by intellectual. The definition proposed by Améry is typical and debatable:

> I certainly do not mean to allude to all those who exercise one of the so-called intellectual professions: having received a good level of education is perhaps a necessary condition but not sufficient. We all know lawyers, physicians, engineers, probably also philologists, who are certainly intelligent, perhaps even excellent in their field, but cannot be called intellectuals. An intellectual, as I would like it to be understood here, is a man who lives within a system of reference which is spiritual in the broadest sense. The sphere of his associations is essentially humanist and philosophical. His esthetic consciousness is well developed. By inclination and aptitude he is attracted by abstract thought. . . . If one talks to him about "society," he understands the term in its sociological but not in its worldly sense. The physical phenomenon that produces a short circuit does not interest him, but he knows all about Neidhart von Reuenthal, that genteel poet of the peasant world.

The definition seems to me pointlessly restrictive: more than a definition it is a self-description, and from the context of which it is a part I would not exclude a shade of irony: in effect, to know von Reuenthal as Améry certainly knew him was of little use in Auschwitz. I would say it is more appropriate that in the term *intellectual* be included, for example, also the mathematician or the naturalist or the philosopher of science; what's more, it must be noted that in different countries it takes on different colorations. But there is no reason to split hairs. We do after all live in a Europe which pretends to be united, and Améry's considerations remain valid even though the concept under discussion is taken in its larger sense. Nor do I wish to follow in Améry's footsteps and pattern an alternate definition on my present condition. (I may be an "intellectual" today, even though the word fills me with vague discomfort; I certainly was not one then, because of moral immaturity, ignorance, and alienation; and if I became one later on, paradoxically I owe that precisely to the Lager experience.) I would propose to extend the term to the person educated beyond his daily trade, whose culture is alive inasmuch as it makes an effort to renew itself, increase itself, and keep up to date, and who does not react with indifference or irritation when confronted by any branch of knowledge, even though, obviously, he cannot cultivate all of them.

In any case, whichever definition one may choose, one can only agree with Améry's conclusions. At work, which was prevalently manual, the cultivated man generally was much worse off than the uncultivated man. Aside from physical strength, he lacked familiarity with the tools and the training, which, however, his worker or peasant companion often had; in contrast, he was tormented by an acute sense of humiliation and destitution. Of *Entwürdigung*, that is, precisely: lost dignity. I remember with precision my first day of work in the Buna plant. Even before adding our shipment of Italians (almost all professional

men or merchants) to the roster of the camp's population, they temporarily sent us to widen a large trench of
clayey ground. They handed me a shovel and immediately
it was a disaster: I was supposed to pick up the loose dirt
at the bottom of the trench with the shovel and lift it over
the edge, which by then was more than two meters high.
It seems easy but it isn't: if one doesn't work with élan,
and the correct élan at that, the loose dirt does not remain
on the shovel but falls off, and frequently on the head of
the inexperienced digger.

Also the "civilian" foreman to whom we were assigned
was temporary. He was a German past middle age, he
gave the impression of being a nice man, and he was sincerely shocked by our clumsiness. When we tried to explain to him that almost none of us had ever held a shovel,
he shrugged his shoulders impatiently: what the hell, we
were prisoners in zebra-striped clothes, and Jews besides.
Everybody must work, because "work makes free": isn't
that what was written on the Lager's gate? This wasn't
a joke, it was exactly so. Well, if we didn't know how to
work, we only had to learn. Wasn't it true that we were
capitalists? It served us right: today it's my turn, tomorrow yours. Some objected and received the first blows of
their career from the *Kapos* inspecting the area, others became despondent; others yet (I among them) confusedly
perceived that there was no way out, and that the best
solution was to learn how to handle a pick and shovel.

Nevertheless, unlike Améry and others, my feeling of
humiliation due to manual work was moderate; evidently
I still was not "intellectual" enough. And after all, why
not? I had a degree, true enough, but mine was an undeserved piece of luck; my family had been rich enough to
send me to school. Many contemporaries of mine had shov-

eled dirt since adolescence. Did I not want equality? Well, then, I had gotten it. I was forced to change my opinion a few days later, when my hands and feet became covered with blisters and infections: no, you can't even improvise at being a digger. I had to learn a few fundamental things in a hurry, which the less fortunate (but in the Lager they were the most fortunate!) learn from childhood: the correct way to grasp tools, the correct movements of the arms and torso, how to handle fatigue and endure pain, knowing when to stop just before exhaustion, at the cost of being slapped and kicked by the *Kapos* and sometimes also by the German "civilians" of the IG Farben works. Blows— I said this elsewhere—generally are not lethal, but collapse is; a punch delivered skillfully contains its own anesthesia, both corporal and spiritual.

Apart from work, barracks life was also more painful for the cultivated man. It was a Hobbesian life, a continuous war of everyone against everyone. (I repeat: this was Auschwitz, the concentrationary capital in 1944. Elsewhere, or at other periods, the situation may have been better, or perhaps even much worse.) The punch delivered by the Authority could be accepted, it was, literally, a case of *force majeur.* Unacceptable, on the other hand, because unexpected and irregular, were the blows received from fellow prisoners, which the civilized man rarely knew how to return. Furthermore, it was possible to find some dignity in manual labor, even in the most onerous, and it was possible to adjust to it, perhaps even by discerning in it a crude form of asceticism or, depending on temperaments, a Conradian "testing of oneself," a recognition of one's limits. Accepting barracks routine was much more difficult: making one's bed in the perfectionist and idiotic manner that I described as one of the useless violences, washing the wooden floor with filthy wet rags, dressing and undressing at a command, exhibiting oneself naked during the innumerable lice, scabies, and personal cleanliness checks, making one's own the militaristic parody of "close order" drill, the "eyes left" and "caps off" briskly executed before the swinish belly of the SS noncom. This indeed was felt as a destitution, a pernicious regression to a desolate state of infancy, bereft of teachers and love.

Améry-Mayer also affirms that he suffered from the mutilation of the language that I described in Chapter 4: and yet his language was German. He suffered from it in a different way than we who, not knowing German, were reduced to the condition of deaf mutes: in a way, if I may put it like this, that was spiritual rather than material. He suffered from it *because* German was his language, because he was a philologist who loved his language, just as a sculptor would suffer at seeing one of his statues befouled or mutilated. Therefore the suffering of the intellectual was different in this case from that of the uncultivated foreigner: for the former the fact that the German of the Lager was a language he did not understand endangered his life; for the latter, it was a barbaric jargon that he did understand but that scorched his mouth when he tried to speak it. One was a deportee, the other a stranger in his own country.

On the subject of blows among companions: not without amusement and retrospective pride, Améry tells in another of his essays of a key episode that should be included in his *Zurückschlagen* or "returning the blow" morality.

A gigantic Polish common criminal punches him in the face over some trifle; he, not because of an animallike reaction but because of a reasoned revolt against the perverted world of the Lager, returns the blow as best he can.

"My dignity," he says, "was all in that punch aimed at his jaw; that in the end it was I who, physically much weaker, succumbed to a ruthless beating no longer had any importance whatsoever. Hurting all over from the blows, I was satisfied with myself." Here I must admit to my absolute inferiority: I have never known how to "return the blow," not out of evangelic saintliness or intellectual aristocracy, but due to an intrinsic incapacity. Perhaps because of the lack of a serious political education: in fact, there does not exist a political program, even the most moderate, even the least violent, that does not allow for some form of active defense. Perhaps because of a lack of physical courage: I possess a certain measure of it when confronted by natural dangers and disease, but I have always been bereft of it when confronted by a human being in the act of aggression. "Trading punches" is an experience I do not have, as far back as I can go in memory; nor can I say I regret not having it. It is indeed because of this that my career as a Partisan was so brief, painful, stupid, and tragic: I had taken on a role that was not mine. I admire Améry's change of heart, his courageous decision to leave the ivory tower and go down onto the battlefield, but it was and is beyond my reach. I admire it, but I must point out that this choice, protracted throughout his post-Auschwitz existence, led him to positions of such severity and intransigence as to make him incapable of finding joy in life, indeed of living. Those who "trade blows" with the entire world achieve dignity but pay a very high price for it because they are sure to be defeated. Améry's suicide, which took place in Salzburg in 1978, like other suicides admits of a cloud of explanations, but, in hindsight, that episode of defying the Pole offers one interpretation.

A few years ago I learned, in a letter to our common friend Hety S., about whom I will speak later on, that Améry called me "the forgiver." I consider this neither insult nor praise but imprecision. I am not inclined to forgive, I never forgave our enemies of that time, nor do I feel I can forgive their imitators in Algeria, Vietnam, the Soviet Union, Chile, Argentina, Cambodia, or South Africa, because I know no human act that can erase a crime; I demand justice, but I am not able, personally, to trade punches or return blows.

I tried to do so only once. Elias, the robust dwarf about whom I spoke in *Survival in Auschwitz* and *Moments of Reprieve*, the man who to all appearances was "happy in the Lager," had, I don't remember for what reason, seized me by the wrist and was insulting me and pushing me against a wall. Like Améry, I had a sudden upsurge of pride; conscious of betraying myself, and of transgressing a norm handed down to me by innumerable forebears alien to violence, I tried to defend myself and landed him a kick on the shin with my wooden clog. Elias roared, not from pain but from wounded dignity. In a flash he crossed my arms over my chest and flung me to the ground, bringing all his weight to bear; then he gripped my throat, attentively watching my face with eyes that I remember very well, at a hand's breadth from mine, fixed, a pale porcelain blue. He squeezed until he saw the signs of loss of consciousness begin; then, without a word, he let go and left.

Following this confirmation, whenever possible, I prefer to delegate punishments, revenges, and retaliations to the laws of my country. This is an obligatory choice: I know how badly these mechanisms function, but I am the way I was made by my past and it is no longer possible for me to change. Had I too seen the world collapse upon me, had I been sentenced to exile and the loss of national identity, had I too been tortured until I fainted and lost consciousness and beyond, perhaps I would have learned to return the blow and to harbor like Améry those "resentments" to which he dedicated a long, anguish-filled essay.

These were culture's obvious disadvantages in Auschwitz. But were there really no advantages? I would be ungrateful for the modest (and "dated") *liceo* and university education allotted to me by fate if I were to deny this; nor does Améry deny it. Culture could be useful: not often, not everywhere, not for everyone, but sometimes, on certain rare occasions, precious as a precious stone, it was actually useful, and one felt almost lifted up from the ground—with the danger of crashing back down again, the pain being all the greater the higher and longer the exaltation lasted.

For example, Améry tells about a friend who in Dachau studied Maimonides: but his friend was a male nurse in the ambulatory, and in Dachau, even though it was a very harsh Lager, there was a library, no less, while in Auschwitz even being able to glance at a newspaper was an unheard of and dangerous event. He also tells that one evening, while marching back from work through the Polish mud, he tried to find again in certain verses by Hölderlin the poetic message which in other times had shook him, but he did not succeed: the verses were there, they sounded in his ear, but they no longer said anything to him; whereas at another moment (typically in the infirmary, after having eaten an extra ration of soup during a respite from hunger) he had been filled with enthusiasm to the point of intoxication by evoking the figure of Joachim

Ziemssen, the mortally ill but extremely dutiful officer in Thomas Mann's *Magic Mountain*.

Culture was useful to me. Not always, at times perhaps by subterranean and unforeseen paths, but it served me well and perhaps it saved me. After forty years I am reading in *Survival in Auschwitz* the chapter entitled "The Canto of Ulysses." It is one of the few episodes whose authenticity I have been able to verify (it is a reassuring operation: after a span of time, as I said in the first chapter, one can doubt one's memory) because my interlocutor of that time, Jean Samuel, is one of the book's few surviving characters. We remained friends, we met several times, and his memories jibe with mine: he remembers that conversation, but, so to speak, without the emphases or with shifted emphases. At that time Dante did not interest him; I interested him by my naive and presumptuous effort to transmit Dante to him, by my language and my confused scholastic reminiscences in the space of half an hour with the soup poles on our shoulders. Well, where I wrote "I would give today's soup to know how to join, I had 'none whatever' to the ending," I had neither lied nor exaggerated. I would really have given bread and soup, that is, blood, to save from nothingness those memories which today with the sure support of printed paper I can refresh whenever I wish and gratis, and which therefore seem of little value.

Then and there they had great value. They made it possible for me to reestablish a link with the past, saving it from oblivion and reinforcing my identity. They convinced me that my mind, although besieged by everyday necessities, had not ceased to function. They elevated me in my own eyes and those of my interlocutor. They granted me a respite, ephemeral but not hebetudinous, in fact liberating and differentiating: in short, a way to find myself. Anyone who has read or seen *Fahrenheit 451* by Ray Bradbury can see what it would mean to be compelled to live in a world without books and what value the memory of books would assume in this world. For me, the Lager was this, too. And before and after "Ulysses" I remember having hounded my Italian companions to help me retrieve this or that tatter of my past world, without getting much out of them, indeed reading irritation and suspicion in their eyes: What is this guy looking for with his Leopardi and the Avogadro's number*? Is hunger driving him crazy?

Nor should I overlook the help I got from my trade as a chemist. On a practical plane, it probably saved me from at least several of the selections for the gas. From what I read afterward on the subject (in particular in *The Crime and Punishment of IG Farben* by J. Borkin), although it was under the jurisdiction of Auschwitz, the Monowitz Lager was owned by the IG Farben Industries, was, in short, a private Lager; and the German industrialists, slightly less myopic than the Nazi commanders, realized that the specialists, to which category I belonged after passing the chemistry exam I was given, were not easily replaced. But I do not mean to refer here to this condition of privilege, or to the obvious advantages of working under cover, without physical labor and without bullying *Kapos:* I refer here to a different advantage. I believe I can dispute, "from personal experience," Améry's statement, which excludes scientists, and therefore with greater justification technicians, from the community of intellectuals. According to him these should be drawn exclusively from the fields of letters and philosophy. Was Leonardo da Vinci, who called himself "a man without letters," not an intellectual?

---

* Number of molecules in a gram molecule.

Together with my baggage of practical notions, I had gotten from my studies and had brought along with me into the Lager an ill-defined patrimony of mental habits which derive from chemistry and its environs but which have broader applications. If I act in a certain way, how will the substance I hold in my hands react, or my human interlocutor? Why does it or he or she manifest or interrupt or change a specific behavior? Can I anticipate what will happen around me in one minute or tomorrow or in a month? If so, which are the signs that matter, which those to neglect? Can I foresee the blow, know from which side it will come, parry it, elude it?

But above all and more specifically: from my trade I contracted a habit that can be variously judged and defined at will as human or inhuman—the habit of never remaining indifferent to the individuals that chance brings before me. They are human beings but also "samples," specimens in a sealed envelope to be identified, analyzed, and weighed. Now, the sample book that Auschwitz had placed open before me was rich, varied, and strange, made up of friends, neutrals and enemies, yet in any case food for my curiosity, which some people, then and later, have judged to be detached. A food that certainly contributed to keeping a part of me alive and that subsequently supplied me with the material for thinking and making books. As I said, I don't know if "down there" I was an intellectual: perhaps I was so in flashes, when the pressure relented. If I became an intellectual afterward, the experience I drew from it certainly helped. I know that this "naturalistic" attitude does not derive only or even necessarily from chemistry, but in my case it did come from chemistry. On the other hand, and it should not seem cynical to say this, for me, as for Lydia Rolfi and many other "fortunate" survivors, the Lager was a university. It taught us to look around and to measure men.

From this aspect, my vision of the world was different from and complementary to that of my companion and antagonist Améry. A different interest transpires from his writings: that of the political combatant who enlisted because of the disease that plagued Europe and threatened (and still threatens) the world; that of the philosopher of the Spirit, which in Auschwitz was absent; that of the diminished scholar from whom the forces of history have stripped away country and identity. Indeed, his gaze is directed on high and rarely lingers on the vulgar populace of the Lager, or on its typical character, the "Muslim," the worn out man, whose intellect is dying or dead.

So then culture could be useful even if only in some marginal cases, and for brief periods; it could enhance an hour, establish a fleeting bond with a companion, keep the mind alive and healthy. It definitely was not useful in orienting oneself and understanding: on this score my experience as a foreigner is identical to that of the German Améry. Reason, art, and poetry are no help in deciphering a place from which they are banned. In the daily life "down there," made up of boredom and interwoven with horror, it was salutary to forget them, just as it was salutary to learn to forget home and family. By this I do not mean definitive oblivion, of which, for all that, no one is capable, but of a relegation to that attic of memory where all the clutter of stuff that is no longer useful in everyday life is stored.

The uncultivated demonstrated a greater proclivity for this operation than did the cultivated. They adjusted sooner to that act of "not trying to understand" which was the first wise dictum one had to learn in the Lager; to try and understand there, on the spot, was a futile effort, even for the many prisoners who came from other Lagers, or who, like Améry, knew history, logic, and morality and, what's more, had experienced imprisonment and torture: a waste of energy that it would have been more useful to invest in the daily struggle against hunger and fatigue. Logic and morality made it impossible to accept an illogical and immoral reality; they engendered a rejection of reality which as a rule led the cultivated man rapidly to despair. But the varieties of the man-animal are innumerable, and I saw and have described men of refined culture, especially if young, throw all this overboard, simplify and barbarize themselves, and survive.

A simple man, accustomed not to ask questions of himself, was beyond the reach of the useless torment of asking himself why; besides, he often had a trade or a manual ability that facilitated his incorporation. It would be difficult to give a complete list, also because it varied from Lager to Lager, and from moment to moment. As a matter of curiosity: in Auschwitz, in December 1944, with the Russians at the gates, the daily air raids and the ice that burst the pipes, a *Buchhalter-Kommando*, an accountants' squad, was instituted; also the same Steinlauf, whom I described in Chapter 3 of *Survival in Auschwitz*, was called to be part of it, although this was not enough to save him from death. Obviously this was an extreme case, to be placed within the general folly of the Third Reich's collapse, yet it was normal and understandable that tailors, shoemakers, mechanics, and bricklayers should find a good position; in fact, they were scarce, and indeed in Monowitz (certainly not for humanitarian reasons) a bricklayer's trade school was set up for prisoners under the age of eighteen.

The philosopher too, says Améry, could arrive at acceptance, but by a longer route. He could perhaps break down the barrier of common sense that forbade him to accept a too ferocious reality as true; he could, finally, admit, living in a monstrous world, that monsters do exist and that along-side Cartesian logic there existed the logic of the SS:

And what if those who proposed to annihilate him were right, based on the undeniable fact that they were the stronger? Thus the fundamental spiritual tolerance and methodical doubt of the intellectual became factors of self-destruction. Yes, the SS were entitled to do what they did: natural right does not exist, and moral categories are born and die with the fashion. There was a Germany that sent Jews and political adversaries to their death because it considered that only in this way could it realize itself. And so? Greek civilization too was based on slavery, and an Athenian army had set up its barracks in Melos just as the SS did in the Ukraine. Human victims were murdered in unheard-of numbers, so far as history's lights can illumine the past, and in any case the perennial quality of human progress was but a naiveté born in the nineteenth century. "*Links zwei drie drei vier*," the *Kapos*' command to mark the step, was a ritual like so many others. There is not much that one can oppose to horror: the Appian Way was bordered by two hedges of crucified slaves, and over Birkenau spread the fetid smell of burnt bodies. In the Lager the intellectual was no longer on the side of Crassus but on that of Spartacus: that's all there is to it.

This surrender before the intrinsic horror of the past could lead the scholarly man to intellectual abdication, furnishing him at the same time with the defensive weapons of his uncultivated companion: "It has always been like this, always will be like this." Perhaps my ignorance of history protected me from this metamorphosis; nor on the other hand, to my good fortune, was I exposed to a further danger that Améry rightly mentions: by his very nature the intellectual (German, if I may be allowed to add this to his pronouncement) tends to become an accomplice of Power, and therefore approves of it. He tends to follow in Hegel's footsteps and deify the State, any State; the sole fact of its existing justifies its existence. The chronicle of Hitlerian Germany teems with cases that confirm this tendency: to it have yielded, confirming it, the philosopher Heidegger, Sartre's mentor, the physicist Stark, a Noble Prize winner, Cardinal Faulhaber, the highest Catholic authority in Germany, and innumerable others.

Alongside this latent propensity of the agnostic intellectual, Améry observes what all of us ex-prisoners observed: the nonagnostic, the believers in any belief whatsoever, better resisted the seduction of power, provided, of course, they were not believers in the National Socialist doctrine. (This qualification is not superfluous: in the Lagers, there were also several convinced Nazis, they too marked with the red triangle of the political prisoner, who had fallen from grace because of ideological dissidence or personal reasons. They were disliked by everyone.) When all is said and done, they also endured the trials of the Lager and survived in a proportionately higher number.

Like Améry, I too entered the Lager as a nonbeliever, and as a nonbeliever I was liberated and have lived to this day. Actually, the experience of the Lager with its frightful iniquity confirmed me in my non-belief. It prevented, and still prevents me from conceiving of any form of providence or transcendent justice: Why were the moribund packed in cattle cars? Why were the children sent to the gas? I must nevertheless admit that I experienced (and again only once) the temptation to yield, to seek refuge in prayer. This happened in October 1944, in the one moment in which I lucidly perceived the imminence of death: when, naked and compressed among my naked companions with my personal index card in hand, I was waiting to file past the "commission" that with one glance would decide whether I should go immediately into the gas chamber or was instead strong enough to go on working. For one instant I felt the need to ask for help and asylum; then, despite my anguish, equanimity prevailed: one does not change the rules of the game at the end of the match, not when you are losing. A prayer under these conditions would have been not only absurd (what rights could I claim? and from whom?) but blasphemous, obscene, laden with the greatest impiety of which a nonbeliever is capable. I rejected that temptation: I knew that otherwise, were I to survive, I would have to be ashamed of it.

Not only during the crucial moments of the selection or the aerial bombings but also in the grind of everyday life, the believers lived better: both Améry and I observed this. It was completely unimportant what their religious or political faith might be. Catholic or Reformed priests, rabbis of the various orthodoxies, militant Zionists, naive or sophisticated Marxists, and Jehovah's Witnesses—all held in common the saving force of their faith. Their universe was vaster than ours, more extended in space and time, above all more comprehensible: they had a key and a point of leverage, a millennial tomorrow so that there might be a sense to sacrificing themselves, a place in heaven or on earth where justice and compassion had won, or would win in a perhaps remote but certain future: Moscow, or the celestial or terrestrial Jerusalem. Their hunger was different from ours. It was a divine punishment or expiation, or votive offering, or the fruit of capitalist putrefaction. Sorrow, in them or around them, was decipherable and therefore did not overflow into despair. They looked at us with commiseration, at times with contempt; some of them, in the intervals of our labor, tried to evangelize us. But how can you, a nonbeliever, fabricate for yourself or accept on the spot an "opportune" faith only because it is opportune? In the fulgurating and very dense days that followed immediately after Liberation, enacted against a pitiful scenery of dying men, dead men, contaminated wind, and polluted snow, the Russians sent me to the barber to be shaved for the first time in my new life as a free man. The barber was an ex-politico, a French worker of the *ceinture;* we immediately felt like brothers, and I made a few banal comments on our so improbable salvation: We were men sentenced to death and freed on the guillotine's platform, wasn't that true? He looked at me open-mouthed, then exclaimed with deep disapproval: "Mais Joseph était là!" Joseph? It took me a few moments to realize that he referred to Stalin. He had not, he had never despaired; Stalin was his fortress, the Rock sung in the psalms.

The demarcation between cultivated and uncultivated, of course, did not at all coincide with that between believers and nonbelievers: indeed, it cut across it at right angles, forming four rather well-defined quadrants: the believing cultivated, the nonbelieving cultivated, the believing uncultivated, the nonbelieving uncultivated; four small jagged, colored islands that stood out against the gray illimitable sea of the semi-alive who perhaps had been cultivated or believing but who by now no longer asked themselves any questions and to whom it would have been pointless and cruel to ask any questions.

The intellectual, Améry notes (and I would specify: the young intellectual, which he and I were at the time of our capture and imprisonment), has drawn from his reading an odorless, ornate, and literary image of death. I translate here "into Italian" his observations as a German philologist, who is led to cite Goethe's "More light!", *Death in Venice*, and Tristan. For us in Italy, death is the second term of the binomial "love and death"; it is Laura's, Ermengarda's, and Clorinda's tender transfiguration; it is the sacrifice of the soldier in battle ("Who for his country dies has lived greatly"); it is "A beautiful death honors all of life." This boundless archive of defensive and thaumaturgic formulations in Auschwitz (and, for that matter, today in any hospital) was short-lived: death in Auschwitz was trivial, bureaucratic, and an everyday affair. It was not commented on, it was not "comforted by tears." In the face of death, in the habit of death, the frontier between culture and lack of culture disappeared. Améry states that one no longer thought about *whether* one would die, an accepted fact, but rather about *how:* "There were discussions about the time necessary for the poison in the gas chambers to take effect. There were speculations about the painfulness of death by phenol injection. Should one hope for a blow on the skull or death by exhaustion in the infirmary?"

On this point my experience and my recollections diverge from Améry's. Perhaps because I was younger, perhaps because I was more ignorant than he, or less marked, or less conscious, I almost never had the time to devote to death. I had many other things to keep me busy—finding a bit of bread, avoiding exhausting work, patching my shoes, stealing a broom, or interpreting the signs and faces around me. The aims of life are the best defense against death: and not only in the Lager.

7
STEREOTYPES

THOSE who experienced imprisonment (and, more generally, all who have gone through harsh experiences) are divided into two distinct categories, with rare intermediate shadings: those who remain silent and those who speak. Both obey valid reasons: those remain silent who feel more deeply that sense of malaise which I for simplicity's sake call ."shame," those who do not feel at peace with themselves, or whose wounds still burn. The others speak, and often speak a lot, obeying different impulses. They speak because, at varied levels of consciousness, they perceive in their (even though by now distant) imprisonment the center of their life, the event that for good or evil has marked their entire existence. They speak because they know they are witnesses in a trial of planetary and epochal dimensions. They speak because (as a Yiddish saying goes) "troubles overcome are good to tell." Francesca tells Dante that there is "no greater sorrow / than to recall happy times / in misery," but the contrary is also true, as all those who have returned know: it is good to sit surrounded by warmth,

before food and wine, and remind oneself and others of the
fatigue, the cold and hunger. It is in this manner that
Ulysses immediately yields to the urgent need to tell his
story, before the table laden with food, at the court of the
king of the Phaeacians. They speak, perhaps even exagger-
ating, as "bragging soldiers," describing fear and courage,
ruses, injuries, defeats, and some victories and by so doing
they differentiate themselves from the "others," consolidate
their identity by belonging to a corporation, and feel their
prestige increased.

But they speak, in fact (I can use the first person plural:
I am not one of the taciturn) we speak also because we are
invited to do so. Years ago, Norberto Bobbio wrote that the
Nazi extermination camps were "not *one of the* events, but
the monstrous, perhaps unrepeatable event of human history." The others, the listeners, friends, children, readers,
or even strangers, sense this, beyond their indignation and
commiseration; they understand the uniqueness of our experience, or at least make an effort to understand it. So they
urge us to speak and ask us questions, at times embarrassing
us: it is not always easy to answer certain whys. We are
neither historians nor philosophers but witnesses, and anyway, who can say that the history of human events obeys
rigorous logic, patterns. One cannot say that each turn follows from a single why: simplifications are proper only for
textbooks; the whys can be many, entangled with one another or unknowable, if not actually nonexistent. No historian or epistemologist has yet proven that human history
is a deterministic process.

Among the questions that are put to us, one is never absent; indeed, as the years go by, it is formulated with ever
increasing persistence, and with an ever less hidden accent
of accusation. More than a single question, it is a family of

questions. Why did you not escape? Why did you not rebel? Why did you not avoid capture "beforehand"? Precisely because of their inevitability, and their increase in time, these questions deserve attention.

The first comments on these questions, and their first interpretation, are optimistic. There exist countries in which freedom was never known, because the need man naturally feels for it comes after other much more pressing needs: to resist cold, hunger, illnesses, parasites, animal and human aggressions. But in countries in which the elementary needs are satisfied, today's young people experience freedom as a good that one must in no case renounce: one cannot do without it, it is a natural and obvious right, and furthermore, it is gratuitous, like health and the air one breathes. The times and places where this congenital right is denied are perceived as distant, foreign, and strange. Therefore, for them the idea of imprisonment is firmly linked to the idea of flight or revolt. The prisoner's condition is perceived as illegitimate, abnormal: in short, as a disease which must be healed by escape or rebellion. In any case, the concept of escape as a moral obligation has strong roots; according to the military code of many countries, the prisoner of war is under an obligation to free himself at all costs, to resume his place as a combatant, and according to the Hague Convention, the attempt to escape must not be punished. In the common consciousness, escape cleanses and wipes out the shame of imprisonment.

Let it be said in passing: in Stalin's Soviet Union the practice, if not the law, was different and much more dramatic. For the repatriated Soviet prisoner of war there was neither healing nor redemption. If he managed to escape and rejoin the fighting army he was considered irremediably guilty; he should have died instead of surrendering, and besides, having been (perhaps only for a few hours) in the hands of the enemy, he was automatically suspected of collusion. On their incautious return home, many military personnel who had been captured by the Germans, dragged into occupied territory, and managed to escape and join the Partisan bands active against the Germans in Italy, France, or even behind the Russian lines, were deported to Siberia or even killed. In wartime Japan as well, the soldier who surrendered was regarded with great contempt; hence the extremely harsh treatment inflicted upon Allied military personnel taken prisoner by the Japanese. They were not only enemies, they were also cowardly enemies, degraded by having surrendered.

More: the concept of escape as a moral duty and the obligatory consequence of captivity is constantly reinforced by romantic (*The Count of Monte Cristo!*) and popular literature (remember the extraordinary success of the memoirs of Papillon). In the universe of the cinema the unjustly (or even justly) incarcerated hero is always a positive character, always tries to escape, even under the least credible circumstances, and the attempt is invariably crowned by success. Among the thousand films buried in oblivion, *I Am an Escaped Convict* and *Hurricane* remain in our memory. The typical prisoner is seen as a man of integrity, in full possession of his physical and moral vigor, who, with the strength that is born of despair and ingenuity sharpened by necessity, flings himself against all barriers and overcomes or shatters them.

Now, this schematic image of prison and escape bears little resemblance to the situation in the concentration camps. Using this term in its broadest sense (that is, besides the extermination camps whose names are universally known, also the many camps of military prisoners and

internees), there existed in Germany several million foreigners in a condition of slavery, overworked, despised,
undernourished, badly clothed, and badly cared for, cut off
from all contact with their native land. They were not
"typical prisoners," they did not have integrity, on the
contrary they were demoralized and depleted. An exception
should be made for the Allied prisoners of war (American
and those belonging to the British Commonwealth), who
received foodstuffs and clothing through the International
Red Cross, had good military training, strong motivations,
and a firm esprit de corps, and had preserved a solid enough
internal hierarchy exempt from the "gray zone" which I
mentioned before. But for a few exceptions, they could
trust each other. They also knew that, should they be re-
captured, they would be treated in accordance with international conventions. In fact, they attempted many escapes,
some successfully.

For everyone else, the pariahs of the Nazi universe,
(among whom must be included gypsies and Soviet prisoners, both military and civilian, who racially were considered not much superior to the Jews), the situation was quite
different. For them escape was difficult and extremely dangerous; besides being demoralized, they had been weakened by hunger and maltreatment; they were and knew
they were considered worth less than beasts of burden.
Their heads were shaved, their filthy clothes were immediately recognizable, their wooden clogs made a swift and
silent step impossible. If they were foreigners, they had
neither acquaintances nor viable places of refuge in the
surroundings; if they were German, they knew they were
under careful surveillance and included in the files of the
sharp-eyed secret police, and that very few among their
countrymen would risk freedom or life to shelter them.

The particular (but numerically imposing) case of the Jews was the most tragic. Even admitting that they managed to get across the barbed wire barrier and the electrified grill, elude the patrols, the surveillance of the sentinels armed with machine guns in the guard towers, the dogs trained for manhunts: In what direction could they flee? To whom could they turn for shelter? They were outside the world, men and women made of air. They no longer had a country (they had been deprived of their original citizenship) or a home, confiscated for the benefit of citizens in good standing. But for a few exceptions, they no longer had a family, or if some relative of theirs was still alive they did not know where to find him or where to write to him without putting the police on his tracks. Goebbels and Streicher's anti-Semitic propaganda had borne fruit: the great majority of Germans, young people in particular, hated Jews, despised them, and considered them the enemies of the people; the rest, with very few heroic exceptions, abstained from any form of help out of fear of the Gestapo. Whoever sheltered or even simply assisted a Jew risked terrifying punishment. In this regard it is only right to remember that a few thousand Jews survived through the entire Hitlerian period, hidden in Germany and Poland in convents, cellars, and attics by citizens who were courageous, compassionate, and above all sufficiently intelligent to observe for years the strictest discretion.

What's more, in all the Lagers the flight of even a single prisoner was considered the most grievous fault on the part of all surveillance personnel, beginning with the functionary-prisoners and ending with the camp commander, who risked discharge. In Nazi logic, this was an intolerable event: the escape of a slave, especially a slave belonging to races "of inferior biological value," seemed to be charged with symbolic value, representing a victory by one who is defeated by definition, a shattering of the myth. Also, more realistically, it was an objective damage since every prisoner had seen things that the world must not know. Consequently, when a prisoner was absent or did not respond at roll call (a not very rare event: often it was simply a matter of a mistake in counting, or a prisoner who had fainted from exhaustion) apocalypse was unleashed. The entire camp was put in a state of alarm. Besides the SS in charge of surveillance, Gestapo patrols intervened; the Lager and its work sites, farmhouses, and houses in the camp's environs were searched. The camp commander arbitrarily ordered emergency measures. The co-nationals or known friends or pallet neighbors of the fugitive were interrogated under torture and then killed. In fact, an escape was a difficult undertaking, and it was unlikely that the fugitive had no accomplices or that his preparations had not been noticed. His hut companions, or at times all the prisoners in the camp, were made to stand in the roll call clearing without any time limit, even for days, under snow, rain, or the hot sun, until the fugitive was found, alive or dead. If he was tracked down and captured alive, he was invariably punished with death by public hanging, but this hanging was preceded by a ceremony that varied each time but was always of an unheard of ferocity, an occasion for the imaginative cruelty of the SS to run amok.

To illustrate how desperate an undertaking an escape was, but not only with this purpose in mind, I will here recall the exploit of Mala Zimetbaum. In fact, I would like the memory of it to survive. Mala's escape from the women's Lager at Auschwitz-Birkenau has been told by several persons, but the details jibe. Mala was a young Polish Jewess who was captured in Belgium and spoke many languages fluently, therefore in Birkenau she acted as an interpreter and messenger and as such enjoyed a certain freedom of movement. She was generous and courageous; she had helped many of her companions and was loved by all of them. In the summer of 1944 she decided to escape with Edek, a Polish political prisoner. She not only wanted to reconquer her own freedom: she was also planning to document the daily massacre at Birkenau. They were able to corrupt an SS and procure two uniforms. They left in disguise and got as far as the Slovak border, where they were stopped by the customs agents, who suspected they were dealing with two deserters and handed them over to the police. They were immediately recognized and taken back to Birkenau. Edek was hung right away but refused to wait for his sentence to be read in obedience to the strict local ritual: he slipped his head into the noose and let himself drop from the stool.

Mala had also resolved to die her own death. While she was waiting in a cell to be interrogated, a companion was able to approach her and asked her, "How are things, Mala?" She answered: "Things are always fine with me." She had managed to conceal a razor blade on her body. At the foot of the gallows, she cut the artery on one of her wrists, the SS who acted as executioners tried to snatch the blade from her and Mala, under the eyes of all the women in the camp, slapped his face with her bloodied hand. Enraged, other guards immediately came running: a prisoner, a Jewess, a woman, had dared defy them! They trampled her to death; she expired, fortunately for her, on the cart taking her to the crematorium.

This was not "useless violence." It was useful: it served very well to crush at its inception any idea of escaping. It was normal for new prisoners to think of escaping, unaware of these refined and tested techniques; it was extremely rare for such a thought to occur to older prisoners. In fact it was common for escape preparations to be denounced by the members of the "gray zone" or by third parties, afraid of the reprisals I have described.

I remember with a smile the adventure I had several years ago in a fifth-grade classroom, where I had been invited to comment on my book and to answer the pupils' questions. An alert-looking little boy, apparently at the head of the class, asked me the obligatory question: "But how come you didn't escape?" I briefly explained to him what I have written here. Not quite convinced, he asked me to draw a sketch of the camp on the blackboard indicating the location of the watch towers, the gates, the barbed wire, and the power station. I did my best, watched by thirty pairs of intent eyes. My interlocutor studied the drawing for a few instants, asked me for a few further clarifications, then he presented to me the plan he had worked out: here, at night, cut the throat of the sentinel; then, put on his clothes; immediately after this, run over there to the power station and cut off the electricity, so the search lights would go out and the high tension fence would be deactivated; after that I could leave without any trouble. He added seriously: "If it should happen to you again, do as I told you. You'll see that you'll be able to do it."

Within its limits, it seems to me that this episode illustrates quite well the gap that exists and grows wider every year between things as they were "down there" and things as they are represented by the current imagination fed by approximative books, films, and myths. It slides fatally toward simplification and stereotype, a trend against which I would like here to erect a dike. At the same time, however, I would like to point out that this phenomenon is not con-

fined to the perception of the near past and historical tragedies; it is much more general, it is part of our difficulty or
inability to perceive the experience of others, which is all
the more pronounced the more distant these experiences are
from ours in time, space, or quality. We are prone to
assimilate them to "related" ones, as if the hunger in Auschwitz were the same as that of someone who has skipped a
meal, or as if escape from Treblinka were similar to an
escape from any ordinary jail. It is the task of the historian
to bridge this gap, which widens as we get farther away
from the events under examination.

With equal frequency, and an even harsher accusatory
tone, we are asked: "Why didn't you rebel?" This question
is quantitively different from the preceding one but similar
in nature, and it too is based on a stereotype. It is advisable
to answer it in two parts.

In the first place, it is not true that no rebellion ever took
place in a Lager. The rebellions of Treblinka, Sobibor, and
Birkenau have been described many times, with an abundance of details; others took place in minor camps. These
were exploits of extreme audacity worthy of the deepest
respect, but not one of them ended in victory, if by victory
one means the liberation of the camp. It would have been
senseless to aim at such a goal: the excessive power of the
guarding troops was such as to cause its failure within
minutes, since the insurgents were practically unarmed.
Their actual aim was to damage or destroy the death installations and permit the escape of the small nucleus of
insurgents, something which at times (for example, in
Treblinka, even though only in part) succeeded. However,
there was never the thought of a mass escape: that would
have been an insane undertaking. What sense, what use
would it have been to open the gates for thousands of in-

dividuals barely able to drag themselves around, and for others who would not have known where, in an enemy country, to look for refuge?

Nevertheless there were insurrections; they were prepared with intelligence and incredible courage by resolute, still physically able minorities. They cost a fearful price in terms of human lives and the collective sufferings inflicted in reprisal but served and still serve to prove that it is false to say that the prisoners of the German Lagers never tried to rebel. In the intentions of the insurgents they were supposed to achieve another, more concrete result: to bring the terrifying secret of the massacre to the attention of the free world. Indeed, those few whose enterprise was successful, and who after many more depleting vicissitudes had access to the organs of information, did speak. But, as I mentioned in my introduction, they were almost never listened to or believed. Uncomfortable truths travel with difficulty.

In the second place, like the nexus imprisonment-flight, the nexus oppression-rebellion is also a stereotype. I don't mean to say that it is never valid: I'm saying that it is not always valid. The history of rebellions, that is, of insurgencies or revolts from below by the "many oppressed" against the few powerful, is as old as the history of humanity and just as varied and tragic. There were a few victorious rebellions, many were defeated, innumerable others were stifled at the start, so early as not to have left any trace in the chronicles. The variables at play are many: the numerical, military, and idealistic strength of the rebels and those of the challenged authority as well, the respective internal cohesions or splits, the external assistance available to one or the other, the ability, charisma, or demonic power of the leaders, and luck. Yet, in every case, one can see that it is never the most oppressed individuals who stand at the head of movements: usually, in fact, revolutions are led by bold, open-minded leaders who throw themselves into the fray out of generosity (or perhaps ambition), even though they personally could have a secure and tranquil, perhaps even privileged life. The image so often repeated in monuments of the slave who breaks his heavy chains is rhetorical; his chains are broken by comrades whose shackles are lighter and looser.

This fact is not surprising. A leader must be efficient: he must possess moral and physical strength, and oppression, if pushed beyond a certain very low level, deteriorates both. To arouse anger and indignation, which are the motor forces of all true rebellions (to be clear about it, those from below: certainly not putsches or "palace revolts"), oppression must certainly exist, but it must be of modest proportions, or enforced inefficiently.

In the Lagers oppression was of extreme proportions and enforced with the renowned and in other fields praiseworthy German efficiency. The typical prisoner, the one who represented the camp's core, was at the limits of depletion: hungry, weakened, covered with sores (especially on the feet: he was an "impeded" man in the original sense of the word—not an unimportant detail!) and therefore profoundly downcast. He was a rag of a man, and, as Marx already knew, revolutions are not made with rags in the real world but only in the world of literary and cinematic rhetoric. All revolutions, those which have changed the direction of world history and those minuscule ones which we are dealing with here, have been led by persons who knew oppression well, but not on their own skin. The Birkenau revolt, which I have already mentioned, was unleashed by the special *Kommando* attached to the crematoria: these were desperate, exasperated men but well fed, clothed, and shod. The revolt in the Warsaw ghetto was an enterprise worthy of the most reverent admiration. It was the first European "resistance" and the only one conducted without the slightest hope of victory or salvation, but it was the work of a political elite which, rightly, had reserved for itself a number of basic privileges in order to preserve its strength.

I come now to the third variant of the question: Why didn't you run away "before"? Before the borders were closed? Before the trap snapped shut? Here too I must point out that many persons threatened by Nazism and fascism did leave "before." These were political exiles, or intellectuals disliked by the two regimes: thousands of names, many obscure, some illustrious, such as Togliatti, Nenni, Saragat, Salvemini, Fermi, Emilio Segré, Lise Meitner, Arnaldo Momigliano, Thomas and Heinrich Mann, Arnold and Stefan Zweig, Brecht, and many others. Not all of them returned, and it was a hemorrhage that bled Europe irremediably. Their emigration (to England, the United States, South America, and the Soviet Union, but also to Belgium, Holland, France, where the Nazi tide was to catch up with them a few years later: they were, as are we all, blind to the future) was neither flight nor desertion but a natural joining up with potential or real allies, in citadels from which they could resume their struggle and their creative activity. Nevertheless, it is still true that for the greater part the threatened families (the Jews, above all) remained in Italy and Germany. To ask oneself and us why is once again the sign of a stereotyped and anachronistic conception of history, more simply put, of a widespread ignorance and forgetfulness, which tends to increase as the events recede further into the past. The Europe of the period 1930–40 was not today's Europe. To emigrate is always painful; at that time it was also more difficult and more costly than it is now. To emigrate one needed not only a lot of money but also a "bridgehead" in the country of destination: relatives or friends willing to offer sponsorship and/or hospitality. Many Italians, peasants above all, had emigrated during the previous decades, but they were driven by poverty and hunger and had a bridgehead, or thought they did. Often they were invited and well received because locally there was a scant supply of manual laborers. Nevertheless, for them and their families leaving their "fatherland" was also a traumatic decision.

"Patria" (that is, "fatherland")—we would do well to examine this term. It is situated quite firmly outside the spoken language: no Italian, except for a joke, would ever say, "I'll take the train and return to the fatherland." The term was coined recently and does not have a single meaning; it does not have exact equivalents in languages other than Italian; it does not appear, as far as I know, in any of our dialects (and this is a sign of its erudite origin and intrinsic abstraction); nor did it always have the same meaning in Italy. In fact, depending on the period, it indicated geographic entities of varying extension, ranging from the village where one was born and (etymologically) where our *padri* (fathers) lived, to the entire nation after the *Risorgimento*. In other countries it is more or less the equivalent of "hearth" or "birthplace." In France (and sometimes also among us) the term has taken on a connotation at once dramatic, polemical, and rhetorical: the *Patrie* becomes such when it is threatened or spurned. For the man who goes away, the concept of *patria* becomes painful and also tends to fade; Pascoli, the poet, having left (not really going very far) his Romagna, his "sweet country," sighed "my *patria* [fatherland] now is where one lives." For Lucia Mondela, the woman in *The Betrothed*, *patria* is visibly identified with the "uneven peaks" of her mountains rising from the waters of Lake Como. By contrast, in countries and times of intense mobility, such as now in the United States and the Soviet Union, there is no talk of *patria*, except in political-bureaucratic terms: what is the hearth, what is "the land of the fathers," of those citizens eternally on the move? Many of them don't know, nor are they concerned about it.

But the Europe of the 1930s was very different indeed. Although industrialized, it was still profoundly agricultural, or permanently urbanized. "Abroad" for the great majority of the population was a remote and vague landscape, mainly for the middle class, less pressed by necessity. Confronted by the Hitlerian menace, the majority of indigenous Jews in Italy, France, Poland, and Germany itself chose to remain in what they felt was their *patria* for reasons that to a great extent they held in common, albeit with different nuances from place to place.

Common to all were the organizational difficulties of emigrating. Those were times of grave international tension: the frontiers of Europe, today almost nonexistent, were practically closed, and England and the Americas had extremely reduced immigration quotas. Yet greater than this difficulty was another of an inner, psychological nature. This village or town or region or nation is mine, I was born here, my ancestors are buried here. I speak its language, have adopted its customs and culture; and to this culture I may even have contributed. I paid its tributes, observed its laws. I fought its battles, not caring whether they were just or unjust. I risked my life for its borders, some of my friends or relations lie in the war cemeteries, I myself, in deference to the current rhetoric, have declared myself willing to die for the *patria*. I do not want to nor can I leave it: if I die I will die "in *patria*"; that will be my way of dying "for the *patria*."

Obviously this sedentary and domestic rather than actively patriotic morality would not have stood up if European Judaism could have foreseen the future. It isn't that the premonitory symptoms of the slaughter were lacking: from his very first books and speeches Hitler had spoken clearly. The Jews (not only the German Jews) were the parasites of humanity and must be eliminated as noxious insects are eliminated. But disquieting deductions have a difficult life: until the last moment, until the incursion of the Nazi (and Fascist) dervishes from house to house, one found a way to deny the signals, ignore the danger, manufacture those convenient truths of which I spoke in the first pages of this book.

This happened to a greater extent in Germany than in Italy. The German Jews were almost all bourgeois and they were German. Like their "Aryan" quasi-compatriots they loved law and order, and not only did they not foresee but they were organically incapable of conceiving of a terrorism directed by the state, even when it was already all around them. There is a famous, extremely dense verse by Christian Morgenstern, a bizarre Bavarian poet (not Jewish, despite his surname) which is quite apposite here, even though it was written in 1910, in the clean, upright, and law-abiding Germany described by J. K. Jerome in *Three Men on the Bummel*. A verse so German and so pregnant that it has become a proverb and cannot be translated into Italian except by a clumsy paraphrase: "*Nicht sein kann, was nicht sein darf*" (What may not be cannot be).

This is the seal of a small emblematic poem: Palmström, an extremely law-abiding German citizen, is hit by a car in a street where traffic is forbidden. He gets up bruised and battered and thinks about it. If traffic is forbidden, vehicles may not circulate, that is, they do not circulate. Ergo he cannot have been hit: it is "an impossible reality," an *Unmögliche Tatsache* (this is the title of the poem). He must have only dreamed it because, indeed, "things whose existence is not morally permissible cannot exist."

One must beware of hindsight and stereotypes. More generally one must beware of the error that consists in judging distant epochs and places with the yardstick that prevails in the here and now, an error all the more difficult to avoid as the distance in space and time increases. This is the reason why, for us who are not specialists, comprehending Biblical and Homeric texts or even the Greek and Latin classics is so arduous an undertaking. Many Europeans of that time—and not only Europeans and not only of that time—behaved and still behave like Palmström, denying the existence of things that ought not to exist. According to common sense, which Manzoni shrewdly distinguished from "good sense," man when threatened provides, resists, or flees, but the threats of those days which today seem evident were at that time obfuscated by willed incredulity, mental blocks, generously exchanged and self-catalyzing consolatory truths.

Here rises the obligatory question, a counter-question: How securely do we live, we men of the century's and millennium's end? And, more specifically, we Europeans? We have been told, and there's no reason to doubt it, that for every human being on the planet a quantity of nuclear explosive is stored equal to three or four tons of TNT. If even only 1 percent of it were used there would immediately be tens of millions dead, and frightening genetic damage to the entire human species, indeed to all life on earth, with the exception perhaps of the insects. Besides, it is at least probable that a third world war, even conventional, even partial, would be fought on our territory between the Atlantic and the Urals, between the Mediterranean and the Arctic. The threat is different from that of the 1930s: less close but vaster; linked, in the opinion of some, to a demonism of history, new, still undecipherable, but not linked (until now) to human demonism. It is aimed at everyone, and therefore especially "useless."

So then? Are today's fears more or less founded than the fears of that time? When it comes to the future, we are just as blind as our fathers. Swiss and Swedes have their anti-nuclear shelters, but what will they find when they come out into the open? There are Polynesia, New Zealand, Tierra del Fuego, the Antarctic: perhaps they will remain unharmed. Obtaining a passport and entry visa is much easier than it was then, so why aren't we going? Why aren't we leaving our country? Why aren't we fleeing "before"?

8

LETTERS FROM GERMANS

Survival in Auschwitz is a book of modest dimensions, but, like a nomadic animal, for forty years now it has left behind it a long and intricate track. It was published for the first time in 1947, a run of two thousand five hundred copies, and was well received by the critics but sold only in part: the six hundred unsold copies stored in Florence in a remainder warehouse were drowned in the autumn flood of 1969. After ten years of "apparent death," it came back to life when the Einaudi publishing company accepted it in 1957. I have often asked myself a futile question: What would have happened if the book had immediately had a wide distribution? Perhaps nothing special. Probably I would have continued my hard working life as a chemist who turned into a writer on Sunday (and not even every Sunday); or perhaps, on the other hand, I might have let myself be dazzled and, with who knows what luck, hoisted the banners of a life-sized writer. As I said, the question is futile: the business of reconstructing the hypothetical past, the what-would-have-happened-if is just as discredited as that of foreseeing the future.

Despite this false start, the book had made its way. It has been translated into eight or nine languages, adapted for radio and theater in Italy and abroad, discussed in innumerable schools. One stage of its itinerary was of fundamental importance for me: its translation into German and its publication in West Germany. When, around 1959, I heard that a German publisher (Fischer Bücherei) had acquired the translation rights I felt overwhelmed by the violent and new emotion of having won a battle. In fact, I had written those pages without a specific recipient in mind. For me, those were things I had inside, that occupied me and that I had to expel: tell them, indeed shout them from the rooftops. But the man who shouts from the rooftops addresses everyone and no one; he clamors in the desert. When I heard of that contract everything changed and became clear to me: yes, I had written the book in Italian, for Italians, for my children, for those who did not know, those who did not want to know, those who were not yet born, those who, willing or not, had assented to the offense; but its true recipients, those against whom the book was aimed like a gun were they, the Germans. Now the gun was loaded.

One must remember that only fifteen years had passed since Auschwitz: the Germans who would read me were "those," not their heirs. Before they had been oppressors or indifferent spectators, now they would be readers: I would corner them, tie them before a mirror. The hour had come to settle accounts, to put the cards on the table. Above all, the hour of colloquy. I was not interested in revenge. I had been intimately satisfied by the symbolic, incomplete, tendentious, modern morality in Nuremberg, but it was fine with me that the very just hangings should be handled by others, professionals. My task was to understand them. Not that handful of high-ranking culprits, but them, the people, those I had seen from close up, those from among whom the SS militia were recruited, and also those others, those who had believed, who not believing had kept silent, who did not have the frail courage to look into our eyes, throw us a piece of bread, whisper a human word. I remember very well that time and that climate, and I believe I can judge those Germans without prejudice or anger. Almost all, but not all, had been deaf, blind, and dumb: a mass of "invalids" surrounding a core of ferocious beasts. Almost all, though not all, had been cowardly. And right here, as a breath of fresh air and to prove how alien I am to global judgments, I would like to recount an episode: it was exceptional, and yet it happened.

In November 1944 we were at work in Auschwitz. Together with two companions I was in the chemical laboratory I have described elsewhere. The air raid alarm sounded and immediately the bombers were visible: there were hundreds, the raid promised to be monstrous. In the camp there were several large bunkers, but they were for the Germans and off limits to us. We had to make do with the fallow grounds, by now already covered with snow, within the enclosure. All of us, prisoners and civilians, ran down the stairs headed for our respective destinations, but the head of the laboratory, a German technician, held us *Häftlinge* chemists back: "You three come with me." Astonished, we followed him at a run toward the bunker, but at the entrance stood a guard with a swastika on his armband. He said: "You can go in; the others beat it." The head of the laboratory answered: "They are with me: it's either everyone or no one," and tried to force his way inside: a boxing match ensued. The guard, who was a strong fellow, certainly would have won, but fortunately for everyone the all-clear sounded: the raid was not for us, the airplanes had continued north. If—another if! but how to resist the fascination of bifurcated paths?—if anomalous Germans, capable of such modest courage, had been more numerous, that time's history and today's geography would be different.

I did not trust my German publisher. I wrote him an almost insolent letter: I warned him not to remove or change a single word in the text, and I insisted that he send me the manuscript of the translation in batches, chapter by chapter, as the work gradually proceeded. I wanted to check on not merely its lexical but also its inner faithfulness. Together with the first chapter, which I found very well translated, I received a letter in perfect Italian from the translator. The publisher had shown him my letter: I had nothing to fear, neither from the publisher nor, even less, from him. He introduced himself: he was exactly my age, had studied in Italy for several years, besides being a translator he was an Italianist, a scholar who specialized in Goldoni. He too was an anomalous German. He had been called up for the army, but he found Nazism repugnant; in 1941 he had simulated an illness, had been sent to a hospital, and had managed to spend his putative convalescence studying Italian literature at the University of Padua. He then had been given a deferral, remained in Padua, and came into contact with the anti-Fascist groups led by Concetto Marchesi, Meneghetti, and Pighin.

In September 1943 came the Italian armistice, and in two days the Germans had militarily occupied northern Italy. My translator had "naturally" joined the Paduan Partisans of the Justice and Liberty groups, who fought in the Colli Euganei against the Fascists of the Republic of Saló and against his compatriots. He had no doubts, he felt more Italian than German, a Partisan and not a Nazi, and yet he knew what he was in for: hardships, dangers, suspicions, and discomforts; if captured by the Germans (and he had in fact been informed that the SS was on his trail) an atrocious death; and moreover, in his own country he would be considered a deserter or even a traitor.

At the end of the war he settled in Berlin, which at that time was not split in two by the wall, but governed by a very complicated condominium regime of the "Big Four" of the time (the United States, the Soviet Union, Great Britain, and France). After his Partisan adventure in Italy he was perfectly bilingual, spoke Italian without the trace of a foreign accent, and began to do translations, first Goldoni because he loved him and because he knew the Venetian dialect well, and for the same reason Agnelo Beolco Il Ruzante, until then unknown in Germany, but also modern Italian authors, Collodi, Gadda, D'Arrigo, and Pirandello. It was not well-paid work, or more accurately, he was too scrupulous and therefore too slow for his working day to be justly recompensed; nevertheless, he could never make up his mind to take a steady job with a publisher. For two reasons: he loved his independence, and besides, subtly, by indirect routes, his political past was held against him. Nobody ever told him in so many words, but a deserter, even in Bonn's superdemocratic Germany, even in quadripartite Berlin, was *persona non grata*.

He was enthusiastic about translating *Survival in Auschwitz*. He had an affinity with the book; it substantiated by its contents his love for freedom and justice, translating it was a way to continue his daring and silent struggle against his misled country. At the time we were both too busy to travel, and a friendly exchange of letters sprung up between us. We were both perfectionists: he by profession; I because, although I found an ally and a valuable ally, I was afraid that my text would lose color, lose pregnancy. For the first time I was caught up in the always burning, never untaxing adventure of being translated, of seeing one's thoughts manhandled, refracted, one's painstakingly chosen word transformed or misunderstood, or even invigorated by some unhoped for resource in the host language.

From the very first installment I was able to see that in reality my "political" suspicions were unfounded: my partner was as much an enemy of the Nazis as I, his indignation was as great as mine. There remained, however, the linguistic suspicions. As I mentioned in the chapter on communication, the German that my text needed, above all in dialogue and quotations, was much coarser than his. He, a man of letters and refined education, did in fact know the German of the barracks (after all, he had had a few months of military service), but *per force* he did not know the degraded, often satanically ironic jargon of the concentration camps. Each of our letters contained a list of proposals and counterproposals, and at times a vehement discussion was set off by a single word. For example, the one I described in this book on page 101. The pattern was general: I indicated a thesis to him, the one suggested to me by the acoustic memory to which I referred before; he presented me with an antithesis, "this is not good German, today's readers would not understand it"; I retorted that " 'down there' we said exactly this"; finally we arrived at the synthesis, that is, a compromise. Experience then taught me that translation and compromise are synonymous, but at that time I was driven by a scruple of superrealism; I wanted that in that book, particularly in its German guise, nothing should be lost of its harshness and the violence inflicted on the language, which for that matter I had made an effort to reproduce as best I could in my Italian original. In a certain sense, it was not a matter of a translation but rather of a resto-ration: his was, or wanted to be, a *restitutio in prisinum*, a retroversion to the language in which events had taken place and to which they belonged. More than a book, it should be a tape recording.

The translator understood quickly and well, and the re-sult was an excellent translation from all points of view; of his fidelity I myself could be the judge, and his stylistic flair was later praised by all reviewers. The question of a preface came up: Fischer the publisher asked me to write it myself. I hesitated, then I refused. I had a feeling of confused re-luctance, repugnance, an emotional block that choked off the flow of ideas and words. In short, I was asked to append to the book—that is, to the testimony—a direct appeal to the German people, a peroration, a sermon. I was expected to raise my voice, climb on the podium, change from witness to judge, preacher; set forth theories and interpretations of history; divide or set apart the pious from the impious; pass from the third person to the second. All these were tasks that went beyond me, tasks I would gladly have delegated to others, perhaps the readers themselves, whether German or not.

I wrote to the publisher that I did not feel up to drafting a preface that would not denature the book, and I proposed an indirect solution to him: to place before the text, instead of an introduction, a passage from the letter which in May 1960, at the end of our laborious collaboration, I wrote to the translator to thank him for his work. I reproduce it here:

And so we are finished: I am glad of it and satisfied with the result, and grateful to you and also a little sad. You understand, it is the only book I have written, and now that we are finished transplanting it into German I feel like a father whose son has reached the age of consent and leaves and one can no longer look after him.

But it is not only this. Perhaps you have realized that for me the Lager, and having written about the Lager, was an important adventure that has profoundly modified me, given me maturity and a reason for life. Perhaps it is presumption: but there it is, today I, prisoner no. 174517, by your help, can speak to the German people, remind them of what they have done, and say to them: "I am alive, and I would like to understand you in order to judge you."

I do not believe that man's life necessarily has a definite purpose; but if I think of my life and the aims I have until now set for myself, I recognize only one of them as well defined and conscious, and it is precisely this, to bear witness, to make my voice heard by the German people, to "answer" the *Kapo* who cleaned his hand on my shoulder, Dr. Pannwitz, and those who hung Ultimo [people described in *Survival in Auschwitz*] and by their heirs.

I am sure that you have not misunderstood me. I never harbored hatred for the German people. And if I had felt that way, I would be cured of it after having known you. I do not understand, I cannot tolerate the fact that a man should be judged not for what he is but because of the group to which he happens to belong. . . .

But I cannot say I understand the Germans. Now something one cannot understand constitutes a painful void, a puncture, a permanent stimulus that insists on being satisfied. I hope that this book will have some echo in Germany, not only out of ambition, but also because the nature of this echo will perhaps make it possible for me to better understand the Germans, to placate this stimulus.

The publisher accepted my proposal, to which the translator had agreed with enthusiasm, so this page forms the introduction to all German editions of *Survival in Auschwitz:* indeed, it is read as an integral part of the text. I became aware of this precisely because of the "nature" of the echo which I allude to in the last lines.

The echo takes material shape in about forty letters written to me by German readers during the years 1961–64: that is, during the crisis which led to the building of that Wall which to this day splits Berlin in two and represents one of the most intense points of attrition in today's world: the only one, besides the Bering Strait, where Americans and Russians directly face each other. All these letters reflect an attentive reading of the book, but all of them answer, or attempt to answer, or deny there is an answer to, the question implicit in the last paragraph of my letter, that is, *whether it is possible to understand the Germans.* Other letters reached me piecemeal during the following years, when the book was reprinted, but the more recent they are, the more pallid they become: the writers are by now the children and grandchildren, the trauma is no longer theirs, it is not being lived in the first person. They express vague solidarity, ignorance, and detachment. For them, that past is truly the past, hearsay. They are not specifically German: with some exceptions, their letters could be confused with those I continue to receive from their Italian contemporaries, so I will not examine them in this review.

The first letters, those which count, are almost all from young people (who say they are or who appear to be young from the contents) with the exception of one, which in 1962 was sent to me by Doctor T. H. of Hamburg and which I present here first because I am in a hurry to get rid of it. I translate its salient passages, respecting their clumsiness:

Dear Dr. Levi:

Your book is the first among the stories by Auschwitz survivors that has come to our knowledge. It has deeply moved
my wife and myself. Now, since you, after all the horrors you
have lived, once again address the German people "to understand," to "awaken an echo," I will dare attempt an answer.
But it will only be an echo; nobody can "understand" such
events! . . .

. . . everything is to be feared from a man who is not with
God: he has no brakes, no restraints! The word from Genesis
8:21 is then appropriate for him: "Because the wisdom of the
human heart is evil since youth," explained in modern times
and proven by the dreadful discoveries of Freud's psychoanalysis in the field of the unconscious which certainly are known
to you. In our times it has happened "that the Devil was unleashed," without restraint, without meaning: persecutions of
Jews and Christians, the extermination of entire populations in
South America, of Indians in North America, of the Goths in
Italy under Narses, horrendous persecutions and massacres
during the French and Russian revolutions. Who will be able
to "understand" all this?

But you certainly expect a specific answer to the question
why Hitler came to power, and why afterward we did not
shake off the yoke. Now, in 1933 . . . all moderate parties
disappeared, and there remained only the choice between
Hitler and Stalin, National Socialists and Communists, whose
forces were approximately equal. We knew the Communists
because of the large revolts that took place after World War I.
Hitler appeared suspect to us, it is true, but decisively as the
lesser evil. That all his beautiful words were falsehood and
betrayal we did not understand at the beginning. In foreign
policy, he had one success after another; all states maintained
diplomatic relations with him, the Pope was the first to make a
concordat. Who could suspect that we were riding (sic) a
criminal and a traitor? And, in any case, no guilt can certainly
be attributed to the betrayed: the traitor alone is guilty.

And now the more difficult question, his insensate hatred for the Jews: well, this hatred was never popular. Germany deservedly counted as the country most friendly to the Jews in the entire world. Never, so far as I know and have read, during the Hitlerian period until its very end, did one ever hear of a single case of spontaneous outrage or aggression against a Jew. Always only (very dangerous) attempts of help.

Now I come to the second question. It is impossible to rebel against a totalitarian state. The entire world, when the time came, was unable to help the Hungarians. . . . Much less could we [resist] all by ourselves. It must not be forgotten that, aside from all the resistance struggles, on July 20, 1944, just on one day, thousands and thousands of officers were executed. It certainly was not a matter of a "small clique," as Hitler said afterward.

Dear Dr. Levi (I take the liberty to address you like this, because anyone who has read your book cannot but hold you dear), I have no excuses. I have no explanations. The guilt weighs heavily on my poor betrayed and misguided people. Rejoice for the life that has been given to you again, the peace of your beautiful country that I too know. Also Dante and Boccaccio have their place on my shelf. Your most devoted, T. H.

To this letter, probably without her husband's knowledge, Frau H. had added the following laconic lines, which I also translate literally:

When a people realizes too late that it has become a prisoner of the devil, from it follows certain psychic alterations.

(1) All that is evil in men is stimulated. The results of this are the *Pannwitzs* and the *Kapos* who clean their hands on the shoulder of the defenseless.

(2) From this results, in contrast, also the active resistance against injustice which sacrificed itself and its family (sic) to martyrdom but without visible success.

(3) There remains the great mass of those who, to save their own lives, keep silent and abandon their brother in danger. This is what we recognize to be our guilt before God and mankind.

I often thought about this strange couple. He seems to me a typical specimen of the large mass of the German upper middle class: a not fanatical but opportunistic Nazi who repented when it was opportune to repent, stupid enough to believe that he can make me believe his simplified version of recent history, and dares to have recourse to Narses's and the Goths' retroactive reprisals. She seems to me a little less hypocritical than her husband but more bigoted.

I answered with a long letter, perhaps the only irate one I ever wrote. That no church offers indulgences to those who follow the Devil or accepts as justification the attribution of one's sins to the Devil. That one must answer personally for sins and errors, otherwise all trace of civilization would vanish from the face of the earth, as in fact it had vanished from the Third Reich. That his electoral data might be good for a child: in the elections of November 1932, the last to be freely held, the Nazis, true enough, obtained one hundred ninety-six seats in the Reichstag, but alongside the Communists with one hundred seats, the Social Democrats, who certainly were not extremists and indeed were detested by Stalin, had obtained one hundred twenty. That, above all, on *my* shelf next to Dante and Boccaccio I kept my *Mein Kampf*, "My Struggle," written by Adolf Hitler many years before coming to power. That dread man was not a traitor, he was a coherent fanatic whose ideas were extremely clear: he never changed them and never concealed them. Those who voted for him certainly voted for his ideas. Nothing is lacking in that book:

the blood and the land, the living space, the Jew as the eternal enemy, the Germans who embody "the highest form of humanity on earth," the other countries openly regarded as the instruments of German domination. These are not "beautiful words"; perhaps Hitler also uttered other words, but he never retracted these.

As for the German resistors, all honor to them but to tell the truth the conspirators of July 20, 1944, bestirred themselves a bit too late. And, finally, I wrote:

Your most audacious statement is the one regarding the unpopularity of anti-Semitism in Germany. It was the foundation of Nazi doctrine from its beginnings: it was of a mystical nature; the Jews could not be "the people elected by God" since that's what the Germans were. There's neither a page nor a speech of Hitler's in which hatred against the Jews is not reiterated to the point of obsession. It was not marginal to Nazism: it was its ideological center. And so: how could the people "most friendly toward the Jews" vote for the party and praise the man who called the Jews Germany's first enemy and claimed that the prime objective of their politics was "strangling the Judaic hydra"?

As for outrages and spontaneous aggressions, your sentence is truly outrageous. In the face of millions of dead people, it seems idle and odious to discuss whether or not it was a matter of spontaneous persecution: and in any case, Germans are not much inclined to spontaneity. But I might remind you that nothing obliged German industrialists to hire famished slaves if not their profit; that no one forced the Topf Company (flourishing today in Wiesbaden) to build the enormous multiple crematoria in the Lagers; that perhaps the SS did receive orders to kill the Jews, but enrollment in the SS was voluntary; that I myself found in Katowitz, after the liberation, innumerable packages of forms by which the heads of German families were authorized to draw clothes and shoes *for adults and for children* from the Auschwitz warehouses; did no one ask himself where so many children's shoes were coming from? And did you never hear about a certain Crystal Night? Or do you think that each single crime committed that night was imposed by force of the law?

That there were attempts to help, I know, and I know that they were dangerous; and in the same way, having lived in Italy, I know "that it is impossible to rebel in a totalitarian state"; but I know that there exist a thousand ways, much less dangerous, to manifest one's solidarity with the oppressed, that these were frequent in Italy even after the German occupation, and that in Hitler's Germany they were carried out much too infrequently.

The remaining letters are very different: they delineate a better world. But I must point out that, even with the best will to absolve, they cannot be considered a "representative sample" of the German people of that time. In the first place, that book of mine was published in some tens of thousands of copies and was therefore read by one out of every thousand citizens of the Federal Republic: a few must have bought it by chance, the rest because they were somehow predisposed to a collision with facts, sensitized, permeable. Among these readers only about forty, as I mentioned, decided to write to me.

In forty years of practice, I have by now become familiar with this singular personage, the reader who writes to the author. He can belong to one of two clearly distinct constellations, one pleasing, the other disagreeable; the intermediate instances are rare. The former give joy and teach. They have read the book attentively, often more than once; they have loved and understood it, at times better than the author himself; they declare themselves enriched by it; they present their views with great clarity and occasionally their criticism; they thank the author for his work; often they explicitly exempt him from writing a reply. The latter are irksome and a waste of time. They exhibit themselves, parade their merits, often have manuscripts in their drawer, and let it become clear that their intention is to climb with the help of the book and the author, as ivy climbs up tree trunks; or they also may be children or adolescents who write out of bravado, on a bet, to obtain an autograph. My forty German correspondents, to whom I dedicate these pages with gratitude, all belong (except for the Dr. T. H. mentioned earlier, who is a case apart) to the first constellation.

L. I. is a librarian in Westphalia; she confesses to having been violently tempted to close the book halfway through "to escape the images evoked in it," but was immediately ashamed of this selfish and cowardly impulse. She writes:

In your preface you express the desire to understand us Germans. You must believe us when we tell you that we ourselves are incapable of conceiving of ourselves or of what we have done. We are guilty. I was born in 1922, grew up in Upper Silesia, not far from Auschwitz, but at the time, in truth, I knew nothing (please do not consider this statement as a convenient excuse, but as a fact) of the atrocious things that were being committed, actually a few kilometers away from us. And yet, at least until the outbreak of the war, I happened to meet here and there people with the Jewish star and I did not welcome them into my home nor did I offer them hospitality as I would have done with others, did not intervene on their behalf. That is my crime. I can come to terms with this terrible levity of mine, cowardice, and selfishness only by relying on Christian forgiveness.

Furthermore, she says she is a member of Aktion Sühnezeichen ("Expiatory Action"), an evangelical association of young people who spend their vacations abroad, rebuilding the cities most grievously damaged by the German war (she went to Coventry). She says nothing about her parents, and this is a symptom: either they knew and did not talk to her; or they did not know, and in that case they had not talked to those who "down there" must certainly have known—the railroad personnel of the convoys, the warehouse workers, the thousands of German workers in the factories and mines where the slave-workers were worked to death, in short, anyone who did not hold his hand over his eyes. I repeat: the true crime, the collective, general crime of almost all Germans of that time was that of lacking the courage to speak.

M. S. from Frankfurt says nothing about himself and cautiously searches for distinctions and justifications: this too is a symptom.

You write that you do understand the Germans. . . . As a German, sensitive to the horror and shame and who will continue to be aware until the end of his days that the horror itself took place by the hand of men of his country, I feel called upon directly by your words and wish to reply.

I too do not understand men like that *Kapo* who wiped his hand on your shoulder, men like Pannwitz, like Eichmann, and all the others who executed inhuman orders without realizing that one cannot evade one's own responsibility by hiding behind that of others. Or that in Germany there were so many material executors of a criminal system and that all this could take place precisely thanks to the great number of people thus disposed and willing, who would not, insofar as they were German, be afflicted by all this.

But are they "the Germans"? And is it permissible in any case to speak "of Germans" as a single entity, or "English" or "Italians" or "Jews"? You mentioned certain exceptions to the

Germans whom you do not understand. . . . I thank you for these words of yours, but I beg you to remember the innumerable Germans . . . who suffered and died in their struggle against iniquity. . . .

With all my heart I wish that many of my compatriots will read your book, so that we Germans will not become lazy and indifferent, but on the contrary that there will remain vivid in us the awareness of how low man can fall when he becomes a torturer of his fellow man. If this will happen, your book will contribute to all this never happening again.

I answered M. S. with perplexity: the same perplexity, for that matter, which I experienced in answering all these polite and civil interlocutors, members of a people who exterminated mine (and many others). What is at stake, essentially, is the same embarrassment experienced by dogs studied by neurologists, conditioned to react in one way to the circle and in another way to the square, so that when the square became rounded and began to resemble a circle, the dogs were blocked and presented the signs of neurosis. I wrote to him, among other things:

I agree with you: it is dangerous, wrong, to speak about the "Germans," or any other people, as of a single undifferentiated entity, and include all individuals in one judgment. And yet I don't think I would deny that there exists a spirit of each people (otherwise it would not be a people) a *Deutschtum*, an *italianità*, an *hispanidad:* they are the sums of traditions, customs, history, language, and culture. Whoever does not feel within himself this spirit, which is national in the best sense of the word, not only does not entirely belong to his own people but is not part of human civilization. Therefore, while I consider insensate the syllogism, "All Italians are passionate; you are Italian; therefore you are passionate," I do however believe it legitimate, within certain limits, to expect from Italians taken

as a whole, or from Germans, etc., one specific, collective behavior rather than another. There will certainly be individual
exceptions, but a prudent, probabilistic forecast is in my opinion possible. . . .

. . . I will be honest with you: in the generation that is over
forty-five, how many are the Germans truly conscious of what
happened in Europe in the name of Germany? To judge from
the disconcerting outcome of a number of trials, I feel they are
few: along with heartbroken and compassionate voices, I hear
others, discordant, strident, too proud of the power and wealth
of today's Germany.

I. J. from Stuttgart is a social worker. She says:

That you were able to prevent an irremediable hatred against
us Germans from seeping through your writings is truly a
miracle and should induce us to shame. For this I would like
to thank you. Unfortunately there are still among us many who
refuse to believe that we Germans really committed such inhuman horrors against the Jewish people. Naturally, this denial
springs from many diverse motives, perhaps even only from
the fact that the intellect of the average citizen refuses to consider the possibility of such profound evil among us "Western
Christians."

It is good that your book was published here and can thus
bring light to many young people. It will also be possible to
put it in the hands of some older people, but to do this, in our
"sleeping" Germany, a certain amount of civil courage is
necessary.

I answered her:

That I do not feel hatred against the German surprises many,
and it should not. In reality, I do understand hatred, but only
ad personam. If I were a judge, even though repressing what
hatred I might feel, I would not hesitate to inflict the most

severe punishment or even death on the many culprits who still today live undisturbed on German soil or in other countries of suspect hospitality; but I would experience horror if a single innocent were punished for a crime he did not commit.

W. A., a physician, writes from Würtemberg:

For us Germans, who carry the heavy burden of our past and (God knows!) of our future, your book is more than a moving tale: it is a help. It is an orientation for which I thank you. I can say nothing to exculpate us; nor do I believe that culpability (*this* culpability!) can easily be obliterated. . . . Much though I try to remove myself from the evil spirit of the past, I still remain a member of this people whom I love and who in the course of centuries has given birth in equal measure to works of noble peace and to others filled with demonic peril. In this converging of all the different times in our history, I am conscious of being implicated in the greatness and culpability of my people. I therefore stand before you as an accomplice of those who did violence to your destiny and the destiny of your people.

W. G. was born in 1935 in Brema; he is a historian and sociologist, a militant member of the Social Democratic party:

At the end of the war I was still a child; I cannot take upon myself any share of guilt for the frightful crimes committed by Germans; and yet I am ashamed of them; I hate the criminals who made you and your companions suffer, and I hate their accomplices, many of whom are still alive. You write that you cannot understand the Germans. If it is your intention to allude to the executioners and their helpers, then I too cannot understand them; but I hope I will have the strength to fight them if they should appear again on the stage of history. I spoke of "shame": I meant to express this feeling—that what was perpetrated by German hands at that time should never have happened, nor should it have been approved of by other Germans.

With H. L. from Bavaria, a student, matters became complicated. She wrote to me for the first time in 1962; her letter was singularly alive, free of the leaden gloom that characterizes almost all the others, even the best intentioned. She assumed that I expected "an echo" above all from important official persons, not from a young girl, but "she feels called upon personally as heir and accomplice." She is satisfied with the education she receives in school, and with what she has been taught about her country's recent history, but she is not sure "that one day the lack of measure that is typical of Germans will not explode again, in a different guise, and directed at other goals." She deplores the fact that her contemporaries reject politics as "something dirty." She reacted in a "violent and rude manner" to a priest who maligned the Jews and to her Russian teacher, a Russian woman who claimed the Jews were responsible for the October Revolution and considered the Hitlerian slaughter a just punishment. At such moments, she experienced "an indescribable shame at belonging to the most barbaric of peoples." "Even though outside all mysticism or superstition," she is convinced "that we Germans will not escape a just punishment for what we committed." She feels somehow authorized, indeed duty-bound, to declare that "we, the children of a generation laden with guilt, are fully conscious of it, and will try to alleviate yesterday's horrors and sufferings so as to avoid their being repeated tomorrow." Since she seemed to me an intelligent, unprejudiced, and "new" interlocutor, I wrote and asked her for more precise information about the situation of the Germany of that time (this was the Adenauer period); as for her fear of a collective "just punishment," I tried to convince her that a punishment, if it is collective, cannot be just, and vice versa. By return post she sent me a card on which she told me that my questions required a certain amount of research; I should be patient, she would answer me exhaustively as soon as possible. Twenty days later I received from her a twenty-three-page letter: in short, a thesis, compiled thanks to a frenzied work of interviews carried out by phone and letter. So this nice girl, too, even though for a good end, had a propensity for *Masslosigkeit*, that lack of measure she herself had denounced, but with comical sincerity she apologized: "I didn't have much time, so many things that I could have said more briefly remained as they were." Since I am not *masslos* I confine myself to summing up and quoting the passages which to me seem most significant.

I love the country where I've grown up, I adore my mother, but despite my efforts the German as a particular human type does not appeal to me: perhaps because he still seems to be too marked by those qualities which in the recent past manifested themselves so rigorously, but perhaps also because in it I detest myself, recognizing that in essence I am like him.

To a question of mine about her school, she answers (with documents) that the entire teaching body was at the proper time put through the sieve of "de-Nazification" demanded by the Allies, but conducted in an amateurish, dilettantesque manner and widely sabotaged. Nor could it have been otherwise: an entire generation would have had to be banished. Recent history is being taught in the schools, but there is little talk about politics; the Nazi past surfaces here and there in varying tones: a few professors boast about it, a few hide it, very few declare themselves immune from it. A young teacher has declared to her as follows:

Pupils are not very interested in this period, but immediately pass to the opposition if one speaks to them about a collective German guilt. Many indeed state that they've had enough of the *mea culpa* of the press and their teachers.

H. L. comments:

It is precisely in the resistance of the young people to the *mea culpa* that one can see how for them the problem of the Third Reich remains just as unresolved, irritating, and typically German as for those who lived before them. Only when this emotionalism has ceased will it be possible to reason objectively.

Elsewhere, speaking of her own experience, H. L. writes (very plausibly):

The professors did not avoid the problems; on the contrary, documenting them with newspapers of the period, they demonstrated the propaganda methods of the Nazis. They told how, when they were young, they had followed the new movement without criticisms and with enthusiasm: youth rallies, sports organizations, etc. We students attacked them strongly, wrongly as I think today: how can one accuse them of having understood the situation, and foreseen the future, behaving no better than the adults? And we, in their place, would we have unmasked better than they the satanic methods with which Hitler conquered the youth for his war?

It should be noted: the justification is the same as that put forward by Dr. T. H. of Hamburg, and at any rate no witness of the time ever denied Hitler a truly demonic talent for persuading, the same talent that favored him in his political contacts. It can be accepted from young people, who, understandably, try to exculpate their fathers' entire generation, but not from the older people compromised and falsely penitent who try to limit the guilt to a single man.

H. L. sent me many more letters, arousing in me bifidous reactions. She described for me her father, a restless musician, shy and sensitive, who died when she was a little girl: was she searching for a father in me? She swayed between documentary seriousness and childish fantasy. She sent me a kaleidoscope and with it she wrote:

About you too I have constructed for myself a well-defined image: it is you who, having escaped a terrifying destiny (forgive my presumption), wanders about our country, still estranged, as in a bad dream. I thought I ought to sew a suit for you like those donned by the heroes of legend, a suit that will protect you from all the world's dangers.

I could not recognize myself in this image, but I did not write her that. I answered that such suits cannot be given away as gifts: one must weave and sew them for oneself. H. L. sent me two novels of Heinrich Mann's *Henry IV* cycle, which unfortunately I never found the time to read; I arranged for her to receive the German translation of *The Reawakening*, which had appeared in the meantime. In December 1964, from Berlin where she had moved, she sent me a pair of gold cufflinks made by a girlfriend of hers who was a goldsmith. I did not have the heart to return them; I thanked her but asked her not to send me anything else. I sincerely hope I did not offend this intimately gentle person; I hope she understood the reason for my defensiveness. Since then I have received no further news from her.

I have left for last my exchange of letters with Mrs. Hety S. of Wiesbaden, my contemporary, because it represents an episode apart both in quality and quantity. By itself, my H. S. dossier is more voluminous than that in which

I keep all the other "letters from Germans." Our correspondence extends over sixteen years, from October 1966 to November 1982. It contains, besides about fifty of her letters (often four or more pages long) and my answers, also the onionskins of at least as many letters she wrote to her children, friends, other writers, publishers, local organizations, newspapers or magazines, copies of which she considered important enough to send me, and, finally, newspaper clippings and book reviews. Some of her letters are "circulars": a half page is a photocopy, the same for several correspondents, the rest is blank and filled in by hand with more personal information or questions. Mrs. Hety S. wrote to me in German and did not know Italian; at first I answered her in French, then I realized that she understood it with difficulty and for a long time I wrote to her in English. Later, with her amused consent, I wrote to her in my uncertain German, in duplicate; she would return one copy to me with her corrections, carefully explained. We met only twice: at her house during a hurried business trip of mine to Germany, and in Turin during just as hurried a vacation of hers. These were not important encounters: the letters count for much more.

Also her first letter took as its point of departure the question of "understanding," but it had an energetic, resentful tone that distinguished it from all the others. My book had been given to her as a gift by a common friend, the historian Hermann Langbein, but very late, when the first edition was already sold out. As cultural assessor of a regional government, she was trying to have it reprinted immediately and wrote to me:

You will certainly never be able to understand "the Germans": even we are unable to do so, because at that time there happened things that, under no circumstances, should have happened. As a result, for many among us words like "Germany" and "Fatherland" have forever lost the meaning they once had: the concept of the "Fatherland" has been obliterated for us. . . . What absolutely is not permissible is to forget. Hence for the new generation books like yours that describe the inhuman in such a human manner are important. . . . Perhaps you do not fully realize how many things a writer can implicitly express about himself—and thus about Man in general. It is precisely this that confers weight and value to every chapter of your book. More than all the rest, I was dismayed by your pages on the Buna laboratory: this then was how you prisoners saw us free people!

A little further on, she tells about a Russian prisoner who during the winter delivered coal to her cellar. Speaking to him was forbidden: she slipped food and cigarettes into his pocket, and he to thank her shouted: "Heil Hitler!" On the other hand, she was not forbidden (What a labyrinth of hierarchies and differentiating prohibitions the Germany of that time must have been! The "letters from Germans" and hers in particular also say more than one might think) to speak with a young French "volunteer" worker: she would pick her up at her camp, bring her home, even take her to a few concerts. In camp the girl was unable to wash herself properly and she had lice. Hety did not dare tell her, she felt embarrassed and was ashamed of her embarrassment.

To this first letter of hers I answered that my book had, it is true, some resonance in Germany, but actually among the Germans who least needed to read it: I had received penitent letters from the innocent, not the guilty. These, understandably, were silent.

In her subsequent letters, little by little, in her indirect way, Hety (for the sake of simplicity I will refer to her like this even though we never reached a first name footing) gave me a portrait of herself. Her father, a pedagogue by profession, was a Social Democratic activist as early as 1919; in 1933, the year Hitler seized power, he immediately lost his job, perquisitions and financial difficulties followed, and the family was forced to move to smaller lodgings. In 1935 Hety was expelled from the lyceum because she had refused to become a member of the Hitler Youth Organization. In 1938 she married an IG-Farben engineer (hence her interest in "the Buna laboratory"!) by whom she immediately had two children. After the attempt on Hitler on July 20, 1944, her father was deported to Dachau, and her marriage underwent a crisis because her husband, even though he wasn't a party member, would not tolerate Hety's endangering herself, him, and the children in order to "do what must be done," that is, take some food every week to the gates of the camp in which her father was imprisoned: "He thought that our efforts were absolutely lunatic. Once we held a family council to see whether there were any possibilities for aiding my father, and if so what they were; but he only said: 'Set your heart at rest: you'll never see him again.' "

Instead, at the end of the war, her father returned, but he looked like a ghost (he died not many years later). Hety, who was very close to him, felt duty-bound to continue his activity in the reborn Social Democratic party; her husband did not agree, there was a quarrel, and he asked for and obtained a divorce. His second wife was a refugee from Eastern Prussia who, because of the two children, kept up a discreet relationship with Hety. Once, with regard to her father, Dachau, and the Lagers, she said to her:

Do not take it in bad part if I cannot bear to read or listen to these concerns of yours. When we had to escape it was terrible;

and the worst thing was that we were forced to go down the route by which the Auschwitz prisoners had been evacuated. The road ran between two hedges of dead bodies. I would like to forget those images and I cannot: I continue to see them in my dreams.

Her father had just returned when Thomas Mann spoke on radio about Auschwitz, the gas, and the crematoria.

We all listened, deeply perturbed, and were for a long time silent. Papa paced back and forth, taciturn, brooding, until I asked him: "But does it seem possible to you that people can be poisoned with gas, burnt, their hair, their skin, their teeth utilized?" And he, even though he did come from Dachau, answered: "No, it is not thinkable. A Thomas Mann should not give credence to such horrors." And yet it was all true: a few weeks later we had proof of it and were convinced.

In another letter of hers she had described their life in "internal emigration":

My mother had a very dear Jewish friend. She was a widow and lived alone, her children had emigrated, but she could not resolve to leave Germany. We too were persecuted, but we were "politicals": it was different for us, and despite the many dangers we were fortunate. I will never forget the evening on which that woman came to us, in the dark, to tell us: "Please, don't come to see me any longer, and excuse me if I do not come to see you. You understand, I would endanger you. . . ." Naturally, we continued to visit her until she was deported to Theresienstadt. We never saw her again and we "did" nothing for her: what could we have done? And yet the thought that nothing could be done still torments us: I beg you, try to understand.

She told me that in 1967 she had attended the Euthanasia Trial. One of the defendants, a physician, had declared in court that he had been personally ordered to give poison injections to the mental patients, and that he had refused because of his professional conscience; by contrast, operating the gas spigot had seemed disagreeable to him, but in fact tolerable. On returning home, Hety found her cleaning woman, a war widow, intent on her work, and her son cooking. They all three sat down at the table and she told the son what she saw and heard at the trial. And suddenly

the woman put down her fork and interrupted aggressively: "What is the point of all these trials they're having now? What could they do about it, our poor soldiers, if they gave them those orders? When my husband came on furlough from Poland, he told me: 'Almost all we did was shoot Jews, shoot Jews all the time. My arm hurt from so much shooting.' But what was he supposed to do, if they had given him those orders?" . . . I discharged her, stifling the temptation to congratulate her on her poor husband fallen in the war. . . . So there, you see, here in Germany even today we live in the midst of this sort of people.

Hety worked many years for the Ministry of Culture of the Land Hessen: she was a diligent but impulsive functionary, the author of polemical reviews, the "impassioned" organizer of conventions and meetings with young people, and just as impassioned about her party's victories and defeats. After her retirement, in 1978, her cultural life became even richer: she wrote to me about travels, lectures, linguistic debates.

But above all, and throughout her life, she was avid, even famished for human encounters: the one with me, durable and fertile, was only one of many. "My destiny drives me toward men with a destiny," she wrote to me once: but more than a destiny what drove her was a vocation. She searched for such persons, found them, put them in touch with one another, extremely curious about their encounters or collisions. It is she who gave me the address of Jean Améry and mine to him, but on one condition: that we both send her carbon copies of the letters we exchanged (we did). She also played an important role in helping me track down that Dr. Müller, the chemist in Auschwitz, later my supplier of chemical products and the penitent about whom I spoke in the Vanadium chapter in *The Periodic Table*. He had been a colleague of her ex-husband's. She also had asked for copies of the Müller dossier, to which she had a right; and she wrote intelligent letters to him about me and to me about him, with dutiful cross-mailings of all copies—"for your information."

Only on one occasion did we (or at least I) perceive a divergence. In 1966 Albert Speer was released from the Inter-Allied Spandau jail. As is known, he had been Hitler's court architect, but in 1943 he was appointed minister of the war industry; in that position he was to a great extent responsible for the organization of the factories in which *we* died of overwork and hunger. At Nuremberg he had been the only one among the defendants to plead guilty, also for things he had not known about; indeed, precisely for not having wanted to know about them. He was sentenced to twenty years' confinement, which he employed in writing his prison memoirs, published in Germany in 1975. Hety at first hesitated, then she read them, and was profoundly perturbed by them. She asked Speer for a meeting, which lasted two hours. She left him Langbein's book on Auschwitz and a copy of *Survival in Auschwitz*, telling him that it was his duty to read them. He gave her a copy of his Spandau diaries for Hety to send on to me.

I received and read these diaries, which bear the mark of

a cultivated and lucid mind and a change of heart that seems sincere (but an intelligent man knows how to simulate). In them Speer comes through as a Shakespearian character of boundless ambition, so great as to blind and contaminate him, but not a barbarian, coward or serf. I would gladly have eschewed this reading, because for me judging is painful, particularly as regards Speer, a not simple man, and a culprit who has paid. I wrote to Hety with a trace of irritation: "What impelled you to visit Speer? Curiosity? A sense of duty? A 'mission'?"

She answered:

I hope you understood the correct meaning of the gift of that book. Your question is also correct. I wanted to look into his face: look at how a man is made who allowed himself to be the succubus of Hitler, and became his creature. He says, and I believe him, that for him the Auschwitz slaughter is a trauma. He's obsessed by the question of how he could "not want to see or know," in short, block everything out. I do not think he's trying to find justification; he would like to understand what, for him, too, it is impossible to understand. He appears to me as a man who does not falsify, fights loyally, and torments himself over his past. For me, he has become a "key": he is a symbolic personage, the symbol of German aberration. He read Langbein's book with great pain, and he promised me that he would also read yours. I will keep you informed of his reactions.

These reactions, to my relief, never arrived: if I had been forced (as is the custom among civilized persons) to answer a letter from Albert Speer, I would have had some problems. In 1978, apologizing to me because of the disapproval she had scented in my letters, Hety visited Speer a second time and came back disappointed. She found him senile, egocentric, pompous, and stupidly proud of his past as a Pharaonic architect. Thereafter the substance of our letters moved toward subjects which were more alarming because more current: the Moro affair, the escape of Kappler, the sudden death of the Baader-Meinhoff terrorist gang in the Stammheim super-jail. She was inclined to believe the official thesis of suicide; I was doubtful. Speer died in 1981, and Hety, unexpectedly, in 1983.

Our friendship, almost exclusively epistolary, was long and fruitful, often cheerful; strange, if I think of the enormous difference between our human itineraries and the geographic and linguistic distance between us, less strange if I recognize that among all my German readers she was the only one "with clean credentials" and therefore not entangled in guilt feelings, and that her curiosity was and is mine, leading her to rack her brains over the same themes I have discussed in this book.

CONCLUSION

THE experiences that we survivors of the Nazi Lagers carry within us are extraneous to the new Western generation and become ever more extraneous as the years pass. For the young people of the 1950s and 1960s these were events connected with their fathers: they were spoken about in the family; memories of them still preserved the freshness of things seen. For the young people of the 1980s, they are matters associated with their grandfathers: distant, blurred, "historical." These young people are besieged by today's problems, different, urgent: the nuclear threat, unemployment, the depletion of resources, the demographic explosion, frenetically innovative technologies to which they must adjust. The world's configuration is profoundly changed; Europe is no longer the center of the planet. The colonial empires have yielded to the pressure of the peoples of Asia and Africa thirsting for independence, having been dissolved not without tragedies and struggles between the new nations. Germany, split in two for an indefinite future, has become "respectable," and in fact holds the destiny of Europe in its hands. The United States–Soviet Union diarchy, born out of World War II, persists; but the ideologies on which the governments of the two sole victors of the last conflict are based have lost much of their credibility and splendor. A skeptical generation stands at the threshold of adulthood, bereft not of ideals but of certainties, indeed distrustful of the grand revealed truth: disposed instead to accept the small truths, changeable from month to month on the convulsed wave of cultural fashions, whether guided or wild.

For us to speak with the young becomes ever more difficult. We see it as a duty and, at the same time, as a risk: the risk of appearing anachronistic, of not being listened to. We must be listened to: above and beyond our personal experiences, we have collectively witnessed a fundamental, unexpected event, fundamental precisely because unexpected, not foreseen by anyone. It took place in the teeth of all forecasts; it happened in Europe; incredibly, it happened that an entire civilized people, just issued from the fervid cultural flowering of Weimar, followed a buffoon whose figure today inspires laughter, and yet Adolf Hitler was obeyed and his praises were sung right up to the catastrophe. It happened, therefore it can happen again: this is the core of what we have to say.

It can happen, and it can happen everywhere. I do not intend to nor can I say that it will happen; as I pointed out earlier, it is not very probable that all the factors that unleashed the Nazi madness will again occur simultaneously but precursory signs loom before us. Violence, "useful" or "useless," is there before our eyes: it snakes either through sporadic and private episodes, or government lawlessness, both in what we call the first and the second worlds, that is to say, the parliamentary democracies and countries in the Communist bloc. In the Third World it is endemic or epidemic. It only awaits its new buffoon (there is no dearth of candidates) to organize it, legalize it, declare it necessary and mandatory, and so contaminate the world. Few countries can be considered immune to a future tide of violence generated by intolerance, lust for power, economic difficulties, religious or political fanaticism, and racialist attritions. It is therefore necessary to sharpen our senses, distrust the prophets, the enchanters, those who speak and write "beautiful words" unsupported by intelligent reasons.

It has obscenely been said that there is a need for conflict: that mankind cannot do without it. It has also been said that local conflicts, violence in the streets, factories, and stadiums, are an equivalent of generalized war and preserve us from it, as petit mal, the epileptic equivalent, preserves from grand mal. It has been observed that never before in Europe did forty years go by without a war: such a long European peace is supposedly an historical anomaly.

These are captious and suspect arguments. Satan is not necessary: there is no need for wars or violence, under any circumstances. There are no problems that cannot be solved around a table, provided there is good will and reciprocal trust—or even reciprocal fear, as the present interminable stalled situation seems to demonstrate, a situation in which the greatest powers confront each other with cordial or threatening faces but have no restraint when it comes to unleashing (or allowing the unleashing) of bloody wars among those "protected" by them, supplying sophisticated weapons, spies, mercenaries, and military advisers instead of arbiters of peace.

Nor is the theory of preventive violence acceptable: from violence only violence is born, following a pendular action that, as time goes by, rather than dying down, becomes more frenzied. In actuality, many signs lead us to think of a genealogy of today's violence that branches out precisely from the violence that was dominant in Hitler's Germany.

Certainly it was not absent before, in the remote and recent past: nevertheless, even in the midst of the insensate slaughter of World War I there survived the traits of a reciprocal respect between the antagonists, a vestige of humanity toward prisoners and unarmed citizens, a tendential respect for treaties: a believer might say "a certain fear of God." The adversary was neither a demon nor a worm. After the Nazi *Gott mit uns,* everything changed. Goering's terrorist bombings were answered by the "carpet" bombings of the Allies. The destruction of a people and a civilization was proven to be possible and desirable both in itself and as an instrument of rule. Hitler learned the massive exploitation of slave labor in the school of Stalin, but in the Soviet Union it was brought back again, multiplied, at the end of the war. The exodus of minds from Germany and Italy, together with the fear of being surpassed by Nazi scientists, gave birth to nuclear bombs. Desperate, the Jewish survivors in flight from Europe after the great shipwreck have created in the bosom of the Arab world an island of Western civilization, a portentous palingenesis of Judaism, and the pretext for renewed hatred. After the defeat, the silent Nazi diaspora has taught the art of persecution and torture to the military and political men of a dozen countries, on the shores of the Mediterranean, the Atlantic, and the Pacific. Many new tyrants have kept in their drawer Adolf Hitler's *Mein Kampf:* with a few changes perhaps, and the substitution of a few names, it can still come in handy.

The Hitlerian example demonstrated to what an extent a war fought in the industrial era can be devastating even without having recourse to nuclear weapons. During the last twenty years the ill-fated Vietnamese enterprise, the Falkland conflict, the Iran–Iraq war, and the events in Cam-

bodia and Afghanistan confirm it. Yet, it has also demonstrated (not in the rigorous sense of mathematicians, unfortunately) that, at least sometimes, at least in part, historical
crimes are punished: the powerful of the Third Reich
ended on the gallows or in suicide; the German people
suffered a Biblical "massacre" of the first born that deci-
mated a generation and a partition of their country that put
an end to century-old German pride. It is not absurd to
assume that, had Nazism not shown itself so very ruthless
from the start, the alliance among its adversaries would not
have been formed, or would have broken up before the end
of the conflict, shattered. The world war willed by the
Nazis and Japanese was a suicidal war: all wars should be
feared as such.

To the stereotypes I reviewed in Chapter VII I would finally like to add one more. More often and more insistently
as that time recedes, we are asked by the young who our
"torturers" were, of what cloth were they made. The term
torturers alludes to our ex-guardians, the SS, and is in my
opinion inappropriate: it brings to mind twisted individuals,
ill-born, sadists, afflicted by an original flaw. Instead, they
were made of the same cloth as we, they were average human beings, averagely intelligent, averagely wicked: save
the exceptions, they were not monsters, they had our faces,
but they had been reared badly. They were, for the greater
part, diligent followers and functionaries, some fanatically
convinced of the Nazi doctrine, many indifferent, or fearful
of punishment, or desirous of a good career, or too obedient.
All of them had been subjected to the terrifying miseduca-
tion provided for and imposed by the schools created in
accordance with the wishes of Hitler and his collaborators,
and then completed by the SS "drill." Many had joined this
militia because of the prestige it conferred, because of its

omnipotence, or even just to escape family problems. Some, very few in truth, had changes of heart, requested transfers to the front lines, gave cautious help to prisoners or chose suicide. Let it be clear that to a greater or lesser degree all were responsible, but it must be just as clear that behind their responsibility stands that great majority of Germans who accepted in the beginning, out of mental laziness, myopic calculation, stupidity, and national pride the "beautiful words" of Corporal Hitler, followed him as long as luck and the lack of scruples favored him, were swept away by his ruin, afflicted by deaths, misery, and remorse, and rehabilitated a few years later as the result of an unprincipled political game.

ABOUT THE AUTHOR

PRIMO LEVI was born in Turin, Italy, in 1919, and was trained as a chemist. Arrested as a member of the anti-Fascist resistance, he was deported to Auschwitz in 1944. Levi's experience in the death camp and his subsequent travels through Eastern Europe were the subjects of his two classic memoirs, *Survival in Auschwitz* and *The Reawakening*, as well as a collection of portraits, *Moments of Reprieve*. Dr. Levi retired from his position as manager of a Turin chemical factory in 1977 to devote himself full-time to writing and was also the author of *The Periodic Table, If Not Now, When?* and *The Monkey's Wrench*. His book *Other People's Trades* and a collection of stories will be published in English next year. *The Drowned and the Saved* was Primo Levi's last completed work. He died in Turin, Italy, in April 1987.

Primo Levi's luminous writings offer a wondrous celebration of life. His universally acclaimed books remain a testament to the indomitability of the human spirit and mankind's capacity to defeat death through meaningful work, morality and art.

ABOUT THE TRANSLATOR

RAYMOND ROSENTHAL is a translator and critic who has been nominated for two National Book Awards for his translations. He received the Present Tense award for his translation of Primo Levi's *The Periodic Table*. He has also brought into English such famous Italian classics as Giovanni Verga's *The House by the Medlar Tree* and Pietro Aretino's *Dialogues*.

VINTAGE INTERNATIONAL

POSSESSION
by A. S. Byatt

An intellectual mystery and a triumphant love story of a pair of young scholars researching the lives of two Victorian poets.

"Gorgeously written . . . a tour de force." *—The New York Times Book Review*

Winner of the Booker Prize
Fiction/Literature/0-679-73590-9

THE REMAINS OF THE DAY
by Kazuo Ishiguro

A profoundly compelling portrait of the perfect English butler and of his fading, insular world in postwar England.

"One of the best books of the year." *—The New York Times Book Review*

Fiction/Literature/0-679-73172-5

ALL THE PRETTY HORSES
by Cormac McCarthy

At sixteen, John Grady Cole finds himself at the end of a long line of Texas ranchers, cut off from the only life he has ever imagined for himself. With two companions, he sets off for Mexico on a sometimes idyllic, sometimes comic journey, to a place where dreams are paid for in blood.

"A book of remarkable beauty and strength, the work of a master in perfect command of his medium." *—Washington Post Book World*

Winner of the National Book Award for Fiction
Fiction/Literature/0-679-74439-8

THE ENGLISH PATIENT
by Michael Ondaatje

During the final moments of World War II, four damaged people come together in a deserted Italian villa. As their stories unfold, a complex tapestry of image and emotion is woven, leaving them inextricably connected by the brutal circumstances of war.

"It seduces and beguiles us with its many-layered mysteries, its brilliantly taut and lyrical prose, its tender regard for its characters." *—Newsday*

Winner of the Booker Prize
Fiction/Literature/0-679-74520-3

VINTAGE   INTERNATIONAL

AVAILABLE AT YOUR LOCAL BOOKSTORE, OR CALL TOLL-FREE TO ORDER: 1-800-793-2665 (CREDIT CARDS ONLY).